MW00655521

Nile Wilson: My Story

Nile Wilson: My Story

Nile Wilson

WHITE OWL

AN IMPRINT OF PEN & SWORD BOOKS LTD.
YORKSHIRE – PHILADELPHIA

First published in Great Britain in 2021 and reprinted in 2022 by
Pen & Sword White Owl
An imprint of
Pen & Sword Books Ltd
Yorkshire - Philadelphia

ISBN 978 1 52677 201 5

Printed and bound in the UK by CPI Group (UK) Ltd, Croydon, CR0 4YY.

Pen & Sword Books Ltd incorporates the Imprints of Pen & Sword Archaeology,
Atlas, Aviation, Battleground, Discovery, Family History, History, Maritime,
Military, Naval, Politics, Railways, Select, Transport, True Crime, Fiction,
Frontline Books, Leo Cooper, Praetorian Press, Seaforth Publishing,
Wharncliffe and White Owl.

For a complete list of Pen & Sword titles please contact

PEN & SWORD BOOKS LIMITED
47 Church Street, Barnsley, South Yorkshire, S70 2AS, England
E-mail: enquiries@pen-and-sword.co.uk
Website: www.pen-and-sword.co.uk

or

PEN AND SWORD BOOKS
1950 Lawrence Rd, Havertown, PA 19083, USA
E-mail: uspen-and-sword@casematepublishers.com
Website: www.penandswordbooks.com

MIX
Paper from
responsible sources
FSC
www.fsc.org   FSC® C013604

I dedicate this book to my Mum, Dad and Joanna.
Everything I do is to make you proud.

Contents

Foreword

'Hi, my name is Nile Wilson and I do roly-polys for a living!'

That has been one of my opening lines on YouTube for so long and I thought it would be a perfect start to this book!

When I first sat down and started writing this book, I wanted the ending of it to be me gloriously holding up an Olympic gold medal at the Tokyo Olympics. I truly felt that was possible but, in the end, it wasn't to be part of my gymnastics journey. But my journey within the sport has been, and still is, about far more than just winning medals. In fact, I feel as though my story is as important now as ever. I have experienced more than most within gymnastics and while the sport is on the cusp of major change, it is time for me to speak my truth.

Most importantly, I want my message to anyone reading this book to be that 'anything is possible' because I am a true reflection of that. When I was 7 years old, we had a new patio put in at our house leading on to the garden. There was a separate side bit where the patio doors were going in where my sister, Joanna, and I could put our handprints into the cement before it dried. My dad asked us both what message we wanted with our handprints, and I said: 'Nile Wilson, Olympic Gymnast'.

That 7-year-old's dream became reality thirteen years later at the Rio Olympics. Within a world in which people are often told to be 'sensible' and protect themselves from possible disappointments, I dreamt big and my parents never shot me down for it. There is a powerful lesson in this. If you're a gymnast shooting for the stars, then understand that the power to achieve what you want already lies within you. You can do this! And if you're not a gymnast then the same message applies to whatever you want to do in life. The world is full of opportunities so get out there and fulfil your dreams. Don't be crippled by fear; be excited about possibilities. As the tattoo on the side of my body says: 'The only limitations in life are the ones we set ourselves.'

My great hope is that this book goes beyond the gymnastics community and is read by people from all sports and all areas of life who experience hardship but still dream big.

I have so many people to thank throughout this book but the first one must go to you for reading this.

Thank you for being part of my journey and remember…

Train Smart, Keep It Real!

Nile

Chapter 1

The Start

My first memory of gymnastics was at Pudsey Leisure Centre when I was 4 years old.

It's all a bit fuzzy in my mind, but I remember the simplicity of the gym with just some mats on the floor and maybe a beam. I also remember walking back to the car afterwards with my mum. So many of my early memories are of my journeys to and from gymnastics with her. I was a high energy and clumsy 4-year-old and fell over and hurt myself on a fairly regular basis. Mum had been a gymnast herself and also a coach; she felt that gymnastics might really help me with my balance and spatial awareness, or at least contain me within lots of soft things so I couldn't hurt myself!

But my first profound gymnastics memory is a summer camp that I went to at Headingley Carnegie University. I guess it is where it all started for me. I genuinely had the time of my life! I got to hang on the rings and the bar and do my first swings and, basically, bounce around on soft cushions; it all felt like a really fun adventure.

Back in 2000, Leeds Gymnastics Club was based at the Carnegie University in Headingley and the summer camp was run by a man called Mike Talbot, or as we used to call him 'Mr T'! He didn't look like the Mr T from the *A Team*, unfortunately, and the bald patch on his head was the exact opposite of the other Mr T's Mohican!

Our Mr T was an amazing man, and I was so lucky to have him involved in my early gymnastics. He had a genuine love for the sport and his passion was infectious. His sessions were always fun and most of the time he worked on a voluntary basis. As time went on, if we knew we had a session coming up with Mr T, there was always an air of excitement with all the kids. He just made us all smile.

It was he who fast-tracked me into being a full member of the club from that summer camp. To get into Leeds Gymnastics Club you would ordinarily need to do well in a regional competition to show you were up to the necessary standard, but Mr T saw something in me on that camp. One day he pointed at me in front of all the other kids and another coach, Chris Lowe (who eventually became Ashley Watson's coach), and looked me in the eyes and said: 'That kid's special. Really special.'

That obviously felt good, but I also felt a bit uncomfortable. I was very young, and everyone was staring at me! I wasn't actually sure if it was good or bad!

I had some very special times with Mr T – he was there when I first learnt to do a dismount off the Pommel Horse. It genuinely brought him as much pride and joy as it did me. Sadly, he was diagnosed with cancer when I was 15 years old and as things started to look bad for him, I went to visit him in hospital. The decline in his health was really rapid and heartbreaking for all of us. In December he was in the office at the club; by January he looked a shell of the man he once was.

Those moments in hospital with him were special, though. I took in my iPad and showed him a pirouetted dismount I had performed that day in the gym off the Pommel Horse. Mr T's face lit up when I showed it to him, and he called in all the doctors to come and see it. There was me, Mr T and five doctors all staring at my iPad in the hospital! Looking back, it was wonderful to have that time with him just before he died. I believe all young gymnasts need an early coach in their lives who will surround them with passion and enthusiasm for the sport. Someone who makes it fun, so you fall in love with it. Mr T was that coach for me.

Mr T's backing meant I was straight into the squad and avoided having to perform at a certain level in a competition to be selected. I have to say, I wouldn't have minded that, but the fast-tracking was out my hands. I was initially assigned a young coach called Andrew Butcher, who I guess was my first proper coach. Obviously, the likes of Mr T had coached me previously, but Andrew was my first serious coach and was dedicated to really progressing my gymnastics. Andrew was a good gymnast himself and we had a good group of us. Everything just felt so exciting and cool at the time in the gym. I just wanted to learn and try everything! It was a bit like being a kid in a candy shop. I was obsessed with learning new tricks and skills, and having a go on each apparatus. By the time I was 8 years old, I had progressed rapidly to doing twenty hours per week of training – Monday to Thursday 5–9 p.m. and Saturday 9 a.m.–1 p.m. Every week. My life was school and gymnastics, while trying to fit in eating and homework as well; I loved it!

Incidentally, at the time, Dave Murray, my eventual main coach, and Tom Rawlinson, my second coach for a number of years, were the young good gymnasts on the scene that I looked up to. They were in the senior squad that I had my eye on! I absolutely loved gymnastics, but I also loved progressing up through the squads; whenever I got moved up a level, I would immediately shift my attention to the level above. That mentality has stayed with me always. I have just wanted to keep progressing and moving forward, whether it be with skills or whichever squad I was in.

With so much of my life dedicated to gymnastics, I would be lying if I said getting my homework done wasn't a battle at times. By the time I got home on a weeknight and had something to eat, it could be 10 p.m. and I was exhausted. However, by the skin of my teeth sometimes, I did always get it done. As well as the odd lunchtime at school, Friday nights at my grandma's became the prime time for me to complete my homework. Although I did get it done, I also did the bare minimum to get by. I just never shared the love that my sister, Joanna, had for learning at school. For me, it was about making sure I didn't get in trouble so I could keep going to the gym as much as possible. So much of my life was dedicated to the gym, but as kids we often forget that means so much of our parents' lives are also consumed by it. They are forever driving you to training or to a competition. Dad did his fair share when he could around work, but it was more often Mum who was driving me to and from gymnastics. In fact, Mum actually started to make the most of that time in the gym.

Mum is a hairdresser and she started to offer haircuts to gymnasts and coaches to make the most out of her time there. While at the gym, guys would step out of the session and get their hair cut and then step back in! The coaches weren't particularly happy about it, but everyone always had sharp hair! There is one particular time – when this whole thing had a huge influence on me – that lives with me till this day. I was about 10 years old and one afternoon my mum went to cut some of the senior squad guys' hair at their house in Headingley. They all shared a house at that time and, as ever, Mum and I went together. While Mum was cutting the boys' hair, I hung out in Dave Murray's room. He had one of those old-school box-shaped computers. None of the ultra-flat iPads, this thing needed its own room! I had never seen a computer like this before, but it was also the first time I was introduced to YouTube. It was 2006 and YouTube was starting to become a 'big thing'. Dave got the beast of a computer fired up and all I did for two hours was watch gymnastics videos. I was immediately hooked. Little did I know how much this would influence me for years to come.

At the time, there were two American gymnasts; twins called Paul and Morgan Hamm. Paul Hamm was the All-Around Olympic Champion from the 2004 Athens games. Both brothers were trying to get back in shape for the 2008 Beijing Olympics and released a training diary on their website, which Dave also showed me. I was fascinated by it; it was so interesting to watch how they prepared, trained and talked about gymnastics. This was just another way for my obsession with gymnastics to shine through. It was another medium for me to absorb information about the sport I was utterly addicted to. My life then became school, gymnastics and watching gymnastics on YouTube, including Paul and Morgan Hamm's training diary. Oh yeah, as ever, I had to fit in eating, homework and sleeping!

I watched every single available gymnastics video on YouTube. The 1996 and 2000 Olympics finals were on there, and I followed every single second of them all, over and over again. I was absolutely obsessed. I remember watching the 2004 Athens Olympics, in particular a Russian gymnast called Alexi Nemov, who was brilliant on the High Bar. He did five release and catch moves, a double twisting, double straight dismount, and I was just blown away. Inspired beyond belief. It is weird to look back on this now and realise how huge these early influences were on me. I watched Nemov and then became a High Bar expert. I got hooked on YouTube and then became a massive influence on there. But above all, I now look back and realise that I got addicted to learning. Learning new skills and the feeling I experienced once I had mastered it. There was no feeling like it for me. That's why I was watching the videos for hours on end, I wanted to learn the skills I was watching. And for me, that is the beauty of gymnastics – there are thousands of different skills and thousands of variations of that skill so there is just so much for you to try and learn. I just loved that. To give a comparison: I have never been able to understand the appeal of endurance sports where there is a limited number of tricks within it. At times, it feels like gymnastics is just limitless in what you can learn.

Every day at training felt like a new science project where I could discover what was possible with my body. However, this was also a science project that brought fear, adrenaline and pain! Trying to master a new skill was scary and physically difficult, but that was all part of the beauty of it. There was this massive thrill to everything. Physically, I am fortunate to have a body for gymnastics – I'm short and stocky – but mentally I also just gravitated to everything that the sport brought.

That early training environment was tough, though; it was no tea party! I loved the sport, but the training was extremely strict. To be honest, it was pretty unnerving at times. Eventually, Moussa Hamani became my main coach – and I never quite knew what to expect from him. It was just the way we were pushed back then. As young boys, we were putting our bodies through a lot of pain to achieve the skills we wanted to master; coaches would push you through that process through discipline and, in truth, some fear. Parents understood the environment as well and it was just the way it was. If you didn't like it, then you would have to walk away. Times have changed, but it definitely needs much more work. This is something I will talk about more in a later chapter, but back then my obsession with the sport carried with it a fear around training as well.

At 9 years old, something happened to me that actually really helped me in dealing with the fear of the training environment. I was diagnosed with osteochondritis of the capitellum, which was an injury to my elbow that meant I couldn't put any weight through that arm for eighteen months. This obviously also meant that my gymnastics became much more restricted, which was really tough to take initially. However, it meant I had more time, so I started playing other sports, mainly cricket and football. I absolutely loved them, especially cricket. I'm lucky to be a natural sportsman so picking up other sports was relatively easy for me. I don't want to sound arrogant, but I was really good at both and the best in my teams. Gymnastics training had given me an amazing physical basis for these other sports. I was the striker in football and was quick, scoring loads of goals. With cricket, I was a fast bowler and an explosive batsman. My body was nimble and fast to react. I was used to learning new skills and loved being in competition. I just really enjoyed these new experiences. I actually felt some relief to have a break from gymnastics, the training culture was so strict that, as much as I was obsessed by the sport, the escape from it felt really good. I even thought I might quit gymnastics, but the end result was actually the opposite.

Looking back, my parents played it really well. They knew how much I loved gymnastics and what my potential was, but they also allowed me the space in this time to enjoy the other sports. We talked about whether I would continue with gymnastics and one night they asked me to write down the positive and negatives of it. We talked about it quite a bit, but deep down I think they always knew I would gravitate back to gymnastics. In the end, the consequences of the injury drew me back to the sport more strongly than ever.

Because of the injury, I was going to the gym only two or three times per week for a couple of hours each time, rather than the twenty or so hours I would have normally been training there. I did what I could in the gym, but it was restricted, and I spent a lot of it watching my group do what I couldn't do. The sessions, the skills they were learning, the progressions they were making, the fun they were having – it was bloody torture! I found it horrendous watching and not being able to be part of it. The strict nature of training seemed a sacrifice worth making to do what I absolutely loved. It was now firmly established in my mind that gymnastics was different from anything else in my life. It was special. It was what I was meant to do. This was what I wanted to do, whatever it took.

Yet, despite feeling like this, I still clung on to wanting to play some cricket down at Farsley Cricket Club on Friday nights. Fridays were my normal day off from gymnastics, so I loved going down and having fun in the nets. I was fully committed to my gymnastics now, but this always felt like a release from the intensity of it. However, this all came to a head on one particular Friday night when I was 11 years old and my elbow injury had fully healed. I was waiting at my grandma's for Dad to take me to cricket, but on that day the national coach, Baz Collie, had come into our gym and asked me to do a session with him. However, I still wanted to go to cricket and have fun. This was quite a big moment. Baz was a very important coach to impress, but I still wanted to have the release of cricket at the end of the week. Looking back, it was another turning point in my commitment to the sport.

Dad arrived at my grandma's and I told him straight away that I wanted to go to cricket instead of the gym. After a little pause, he replied that I was either training with Baz or we were going home. My response: 'Let's go home then.'

There and then, I hated my dad for the choice he was forcing me to make. We went home and Dad immediately started gardening. I was left to think about what I wanted to do and I sure as hell didn't just want to be sitting at home! It didn't take long for me to walk into the garden and ask Dad to take me to the gym, which he did straight away. We have spoken a lot about this incident in recent years because it was definitely a 'sliding doors' moment in my life. He's explained that he knew how talented I was and how much I loved gymnastics. He didn't want me to come back to him when I was 20 years old and tell him how much I wished he had forced me to go to the gym that night. In the end, it wasn't about him forcing me to go to the gym, it was about him putting me in a position where I had to make the decision with cricket taken out of the equation. The decision to go to the gym was all mine and I am forever grateful for that.

I arrived at the gym with a long face but came out so happy. I absolutely loved it! Baz and I have always had a massive connection and the session was brilliant. It was fun, exciting and challenging. Over time, I would learn more and more just how far Baz could push sessions and he did this day. It was exhilarating. Afterwards, I thanked my dad for giving me that much-needed push. From that day on, it was only gymnastics in my life, all the other sports were left behind.

Even though I loved gymnastics, for the next couple of years I still needed to be pushed to go to training once in a while, especially when I was tired. I was also pushed at training and always told what to do; I followed the instructions of my coaches. However, at around the age of 14, all this changed. There was a switch in me and suddenly I was doing it all for me. I wanted to do it all. I began pushing myself at training and no longer needed to be told what to do. There was no debate on whether to go to the odd training session – I wanted to go to every single one – and there was most definitely no more talk of me quitting gymnastics.

This switch in my mentality coincided with me starting to compete more, and, importantly, win. In fact, this could have absolutely contributed to that switch. I loved the environment of competition and the attention it brought. I loved performing a routine that I had grafted to master and then absolutely nail a good score with. It was like the icing on the cake and that buzz has always lived with me. I was thriving in that environment.

Indeed, after a full year out from my injury, I won six gold medals at the British Championships and became Under-12's British Champion. That fast-tracked me to my first international. It was during these two years, as I came through my injury and turned 14, when it became clear to everyone, including me, that I was the real deal. I could be something special in gymnastics. My coaches all knew it and I felt it inside. I was the perfect balance of a lot of different elements that made for a potentially great gymnast. Physiologically, I was perfect for gymnastics: short, strong and fast. Mentally, I loved both training and competing, which can be different for other people. Some guys hate training but love competing, yet I was obsessed with learning and putting myself out of my comfort zone. I loved training and wanted to do it as smartly as I good, which is where my catchphrase 'Train Smart, Keep It Real' came from. And I loved performing on the stage. I thrived in competition, whereas I know other guys who loved training but found the pressure of competition too much.

In many ways, I was a perfect storm for gymnastics, and it was clear that I had massive potential in the sport.

Behind the scenes, all of my progression to this point and then beyond it felt as though it was building towards the 2012 European Junior Championships in France. The team was led by Baz Collie and it was to be a competition I would never forget – for both good and bad reasons.

Chapter 2

Elite Junior Gymnastics

It felt as though every progression I had made since I was that 4-year-old walking into Pudsey Leisure Centre was directed towards the 2012 European Junior Championships in Montpellier, France, when I was 16 years old.

OK, it wasn't the Olympic Games, but at that point in my gymnastics career it felt like a mini crescendo that everything had been building towards. It turned out to be a pivotal moment in my career, the first major junior international competition and one I will never forget – for both good and bad reasons. Unfortunately, the bad outweighed the good.

Baz Collie was our head coach and his focus on us doing well at this competition was ferocious. His intensity around us winning was like nothing else and it fed down to the gymnasts. We were under enormous pressure and there was very little fun involved; it was all about the outcome. Baz was, and is, a brilliant coach and person, but this competition also proved to be a crucial moment in his coaching career.

We won the team competition, which is what all the focus was about; I won silver in the All-Around, behind my teammate Frank Baines, and also made the High Bar final. This was a big step forward for me in delivering in my first major competition. Although the results were what everyone wanted, I just didn't enjoy it at all because the pressure on the outcomes was suffocating. I learnt that I didn't react well to that environment and it was the first signs of the issues I would have with my weight and an eating disorder.

I became obsessed about losing weight under the belief that the lighter I was, the better I would be. In the three months running up to these championships, I lost nearly 10kgs: 61kgs to 52kgs, it was total madness. I was barely eating. I was already small, but then this dramatic weight loss left me feeling weak physically but also, crucially, mentally.

It was around this time that my issues with binge eating were at their worst. To some people they will think binge eating is just someone overindulging who needs to control themselves, but it is much more serious than that. I have learnt that it is an eating disorder and a mental health issue. I wrote about this in my first book, but I repeat it here as it is so important for people to understand what happens to someone suffering with binge eating.

I would be very disciplined with my eating for a period of time, to the point of the extreme, not touching anything that I 'believed' would make me put on weight. I put 'believed' in inverted commas because I wouldn't be thinking rationally about this. I would barely eat or not eat anywhere near enough calories to keep myself healthy for the level of activity I accomplished. And, throughout all of this, I was like a pressure cooker building up. The focus on what I should and should not eat would be so intense and eventually I would blow. Once that happened, I was out of control. Two or three hours could go by without me really knowing what had happened. It was just about me eating more and more and more. My stomach would be uncomfortably full, having eaten four or five times more food that I needed. This was not about eating a bit too much chocolate or an extra bowl of ice cream, this was much more extreme eating until, at times, 3 a.m. It was horrible.

Then shame and massive guilt would hit me. 'Why have I done this?' 'How did this happen?' It would have a hugely negative impact on the next few days ahead. I would then believe that I had to solve the problem I had created and hardly eat at all for a few days while trying to train hard. And then again, the pressure cooker would be building up and bang ... it would happen again. I'd be back in the vicious cycle.

Much of this centred on weekends – when things would go wrong. Monday, Tuesday and Wednesday would be average days in the gym after a binge. At times I could weigh 3 or 4 kilos heavier than normal and might struggle to train properly. I would then wrestle things back towards the end of the week before bingeing again at the weekend – and it would all begin again. It was as if I was inside a spinning record player and couldn't get out.

But please don't get me wrong, Baz was not responsible for this; it was my own demons in dealing with pressure at that time in my life, although the team environment we took to Montpellier was not a healthy one. It got results, but for what? I know that Baz reflects back on Montpellier as a turning point for him as a coach. He achieved the results he had pushed so hard for, but was left with an empty feeling afterwards. After Montpellier, both he and I realised that the beauty in what we do as gymnast and coach is in the fun of the journey. The results will take care of themselves, but the more important thing is the enjoyment and adventure we get in trying to learn new things and pushing our skills levels to the maximum. That is what gives us a long-lasting sense of fulfilment. If we hyper focus on outcomes, we lose sight of why we are truly in love with our sport.

Two years later, at the 2014 European Junior Championships in Sofia, Bulgaria, things couldn't have been more different. OK, I was 18, the captain and senior member of the team and had a weight of expectation around me, but our whole team environment was so much happier and healthier. Baz was head coach again and completely shifted his style from two years earlier in Montpellier. Still to this day, Sofia is one of my happiest memories in gymnastics and I am so grateful for the changes Baz made. We were happy and healthy and guess what? We made history! I won five gold medals and absolutely smashed it. We won the team event and I also won All-Around, Parallel Bars, High Bar and, wait for it ... Pommel Horse! It just proved that the results would take care of themselves in a good environment.

In Sofia, I knew it was my time. I knew my skills and my body; I was truly coming of age. I could sense that I was moving up a level with my gymnastics. I had to deliver in this competition, and I nailed it, though not without problems. I qualified in first for the All-Around final and felt that I was favourite to win. My first piece in the final was the Vault in which I performed reasonably. I still felt great, however, early in my next piece, the Parallel Bars, I sat on the bar during a move called the Tipelt. That cost me a mark and I was lying in thirteenth place after the second rotation. To some people that could have been disastrous and the end of their challenge as they crumbled mentally, but I clearly remember believing that I could still win. My attitude was that I could smash all of my next routines and still take gold. I was determined, focused and most importantly, undeterred from my mistake on the Parallel Bars. In the end I won gold after following up the mistake with four of my best routines as a junior gymnast on the next four pieces. It was a magic moment for me.

To put my skill level at this time in some context here, I wasn't doing baby junior skills, I was already performing at a level that would challenge medals at the senior level. I was most definitely ready to land on the map with the senior competitions. And, boom, three months later I was picked for the 2014 Commonwealth Games in Glasgow. It was another huge step for me. The team was also made up of all the guys from the London 2012 Olympics: Max Whitlock, Sam Oldham, Louis Smith and Kristian Thomas. All had serious pedigrees that I looked up to. This was a whole different ball game, and I was a baby amongst these guys. Everything at Glasgow felt completely different from anything I had experienced before.

I will never forget the feeling when I first walked out on to the arena – the roar was huge! I actually felt sick! But behind all of this, I also had a feeling that this was where I belonged. I enjoyed the attention that these stages gave me. This was for me.

There had been so many important moments in my career before Glasgow, but those games were a game changer for me at a senior level. I was 18, a relative baby compared to others, and I won a bronze medal in the All-Around behind Dan Keatings and Max Whitlock. Everyone was gobsmacked with the way I performed, including all the coaches. Everyone knew then that this baby could handle the major competitions and, with two years until the next Olympics, other gymnasts now knew I was a real threat.

I took the Commonwealth Games in my stride and the next major event on the horizon was the World Championships in October in China. Originally, the thought from the coaches was that I would go to China as a reserve and just gain some valuable experience. However, with Sam Oldham's injury on the Vault at Glasgow, everything changed. After the way I performed in Glasgow, they needed me in the team. This was obviously brilliant, but there was one major downside: it scuppered my first ever lads' holiday to Kavos! The holiday was going to clash with my preparations for the Worlds and everyone at the time told me it wasn't a goer. Initially, I actually took it really badly. So much had been happening for me in the last few months that I was really looking forward to a release of the pressure on the holiday. After the massive high of Glasgow, I cried and cried, I was a wreck about it! It was obviously the right thing not to go but it hurt at the time.

The World Championships in China was another huge step up for me. This was truly the world stage and far beyond the Commonwealth Games in Glasgow. I guess everyone was watching to see how I would perform. My potential and talent weren't in question, but there is always an unknown as to how a very young sportsperson will react on that stage. I was also carrying an injury in the championships. My wrist had been hurting badly for two weeks running up to it, and it got so painful that it was decided I would have local anaesthetic injections in it to get through. We tested this with an injection in training and then another for Podium Training; and it worked brilliantly! I felt zero pain, it was mind-blowing really. I smashed Qualification, hitting everything and actually qualified ahead of Max Whitlock for the All-Around final. I also qualified for the High Bar final.

I was still only 18 years old, in my first World Championships and with a dodgy wrist, yet I was stepping up big time. My confidence just skyrocketed. I now knew without any doubt at all that on the big stage, I could deliver. And this wasn't just from the Worlds, it was from every routine I had performed: from the European Juniors in Sofia to the Commonwealth Games in Glasgow and now to the World Championships in China. I was nailing it, again and again. My self-belief was becoming rock solid.

Unfortunately, my wrist injury wasn't finished with me. During the team event, as we chased Japan, China and the USA for a medal, the injection stopped working. I could feel a lot of pain in my wrist. Despite this, I did four pieces and scored 15 in both the High Bar and Parallel Bars. Although we disappointingly missed out on a medal, my performance under pain was still excellent. My wrist was a worry though, especially ahead of the All-Around final which was yet to come.

When I woke up the next day, my wrist was a 10/10 pain. It was excruciating. I met with the team doctor and Baz, and it was decided I couldn't take part in the All-Around final. As devastating as this was, the pain was so intense that I knew this was the right decision. The funnier part of this all was when Max Whitlock was told that he would replace me in the final; I walked into one of the lads' rooms and Max was putting a slice of pizza into his mouth as I told him that I was out, and he was in! He dropped the pizza in total shock. Fair play to Max, he went on to win silver in the final.

The High Bar final, which I had also qualified for, was four days later and so with longer recovery time, I was able to compete in it. I ended up coming fourth, which again was a massive achievement. China was a huge marker for me on what I could do at world level. The Rio Olympics were two years away and everyone knew I was getting into pole position to be selected for them. However, there was still the problem of my wrist.

After returning home, it was diagnosed that I had ripped the cartilage off the bone and needed surgery. It would be a six-month rehabilitation. I had been untouchable for all of 2014 until now. This injury was the first major stumbling block I had experienced as an international gymnast. It was far enough away from Rio to be OK, but it was still a big issue for me to overcome.

In the end, it was eight months before I competed again. It was a very long eight months and I hated being away from competition. Once the injury was fully healed, Dave Murray (my Leeds Gymnastics Club coach then) and I worked on my routines to develop my skill level further. We wanted to achieve bigger routines. It was a good time to do it but changes to your routines always take time to fully master. It's all good and well doing it in training under no pressure, but it's a different thing nailing it in the heat of a competition. You simply need the training time under your belt.

And that's why the European Games in Baku, Azerbaijan in 2015 were a total shocker. In 2014, I was a weathered performer, competing regularly and with total mastery of my routines. After eight months away from competition, I arrived in Baku in a very different situation and made a load of mistakes. I didn't qualify for any finals. I was rusty and maybe a little naive in expecting all the changes to my routines to be mastered in such a short period. It was a learning experience, but with about a year to the Rio Olympics, it did get me a little worried. Could I get back to the Nile of 2014 and have that unshakeable confidence in my routines and my ability to step up on the big stage?

Thankfully, the 2015 London Open proved to me that I could. After Baku, Dave and I spent hours in the gym to achieve that mastery of all the changes I had made to my routines. There was just no substitute for that time in the gym. The London Open was the official trials for the World Championships in October in Glasgow, and I smashed it. I scored 89 in the All-Around, coming second behind Max Whitlock and therefore qualifying for the Worlds. The cobwebs from Baku were well and truly gone and I knew I was back.

After the Commonwealth Games in 2014, Glasgow was a favourite venue of mine and it was brilliant to be back there for the World

Championships. The energy off the crowd there was always amazing. I felt confident and ready to perform, and sure enough, I did. We also performed brilliantly as a team and took silver in the team event, immediately qualifying for the Olympics. It was a huge moment. From the 2014 European Junior Championships, my journey had felt incredible. So much had happened over those last two years – moving from juniors to seniors, winning medals everywhere, my first major injury requiring surgery but, most importantly, the building of a rock-solid self-belief that on the big stages, I could deliver. As I stood with the rest of the team celebrating our medal at the World Championships, I knew that the possibility of me going to the Rio Olympics and doing well was very real. It was within my grasp. However, there was something going on behind the scenes that had the potential to undermine everything.

In the run up to the World Championships I picked up a shoulder injury that required me to rest up for two weeks. It was nothing major, but with only twelve weeks before the championships, it wasn't ideal. This mini break gave me time away from the gym. Time on my own, getting bored, and wanting to find ways to entertain my busy mind. It started with online gambling. Just a little bit at a time, but it continued when I was back in full training. Online progressed to me actually going to the casino three or four times a week. It just seemed to grow on me from nowhere. One minute I was just playing with small amounts of money online; the next minute I was standing at the end of the Vault run up and all I was thinking about was the roulette wheel. The addiction's escalation was rapid.

One night during a British squad training week at Lilleshall, I stayed up till 3 a.m. playing roulette. I couldn't stop and I lost £800, which for me at the time was a large sum of money. I was devastated and frightened. I looked in the mirror and just cried my eyes out. This wasn't the first time it had happened, and it was terrifying that I couldn't just stop it. After every episode like this, I would wake up next morning and have about five seconds of bliss, and then I would remember what I had done the night before. The shame and stress would hit me like a ton of bricks. *What was I doing to myself?*

And this was all going on during the run up to a World Championships from which Olympic team selection came. I had done so much to this point in my gymnastics and yet I was causing myself so much pressure from something away from the gym that I had lost control of. I was earning £20,000 a year at the time, and I lost about £5,000 in six months. It was money I just didn't have. I would be paid at the end of the month and then blow all my money and have £50 to survive for two weeks. I was training as an elite athlete but had this stress hanging over me. It was like a silent killer in my life.

I just couldn't take it any more and did the best thing I could do in that situation: reached out for help. I talked to the British Gymnastics' psychologist, Gemma, and then told Baz. It was terrifying, especially with Baz, but also a massive relief. I just couldn't deal with it myself and couldn't get out of the hole I had dug for myself.

Gemma and Baz were amazing and we agreed that the next step was to tell my parents. Baz lived in Leeds and was going to drop me off at home after the camp anyway, so we agreed that he would come with me when I told them. I was absolutely petrified about how my parents would react. I was shaking and crying and couldn't have done it without Baz there.

My parents paused and then just smiled and gave me a huge hug. The relief poured from me. My secret was out now so I didn't need to lie any more. I was now also accountable to all these people that mattered so much to me and that in itself would stop me. And it really did. By reaching out and admitting my problem, I stopped the gambling.

From that point, I didn't look back in my run-in to the Olympics. From February to August, I was like a competing machine. I travelled everywhere to compete. At the European Championships in Bern

I scored 89.8 and won the High Bar, which was my first senior title; I even went to Rio to take part in a test event at the Olympic venue. By the time I scored 89 in the Olympic All-Around final, it was the thirteenth time I had scored 89 or more since February. I was so well tuned, fit and consistent.

I was ready for my first Olympic experience.

Chapter 3

2016 Rio Olympics

I once asked Louis Smith what it felt like to be in an Olympic Games, and he said the feeling was something so intense that you could never prepare for it. He was 100 per cent right.

From the age of 4, I had dedicated my whole life towards this and now here I was at the 2016 Rio Olympic Games. As I arrived at the Olympic Village, along with the rest of Team GB, it was surreal and brilliant, all wrapped into one. I had to pinch myself at times. The Olympic Village was like a city with big tower apartment blocks for different teams and a food hall that seated 5,000. You could have any food or drink you wanted – all for free! There was even a McDonald's in the village. In fact, the 'getting everything for free' thing nearly got me into trouble when I got back to Leeds and walked out of my local One-Stop having grabbed a can of Coke from the fridge! Don't worry, when the alarm went off in the shop, I realised what I had done.

Sporting superstars just casually strolled around the village, but the thing was that we were all just the same. We had all dedicated our lives to be there, we had all been on the same journey, so the mutual respect was immediate. I bumped into Andy Murray in the lift after a couple of days and I was a bit shocked at first, but we started chatting straight away and I then realised that there was this connection between the athletes – he was just a tennis player and I was just a gymnast, both representing Team GB in an Olympic Games. We were teammates and friends straight away. It was so special and blew me away at times.

I shared a room with Bryn Evans and an apartment with some of my other teammates, including Louis Smith – it was absolutely brilliant. We had this incredible feeling of camaraderie – we were sharing this mind-blowing experience. We had a balcony and most of the apartment blocks had their own outdoor pool because the climate was so good. I just loved all of it. In fact, the only difficult thing at the start was killing time and conserving energy. We had arrived about a week before competing so that we could acclimatise. We trained in the mornings, so once training was done there was the whole afternoon and evening to kill. It was just about recovering, eating and sleeping to perfection, which we did down to the last detail, but we did need to pace ourselves in the run-up to competing. With the excitement of being there and there being so much to absorb and see, we needed to be careful not to burn too much nervous energy. We could end up being exhausted by the time it came to competing.

As with all major gymnastic events, we had Podium Training two days before the Qualification events. This is where you do your full routines inside the Olympic Arena. The judges sit in on it and you present to them and your coaches. It's like a dress rehearsal and quite a tricky one at that. You might want to look good during it but there is not the adrenaline buzz you get from a live competition, and it is vital to conserve energy with only two days to go. It can often be a little bit bumpy as you just want to be ticking over so that when it is time to compete, you are at your peak. I was solid during Podium Training – a couple of small mistakes to tighten up for the competition, but I was on top of everything.

When the day came for us to compete in the Team Qualification event, I was at my absolute peak – I felt brilliant and smashed it. I scored 89.5 in the All-Around, qualifying fourth for the final, and 15.5 on the High Bar to qualify second for the final. As a team, we were also comfortably in the final. At this stage, I didn't really have any big thoughts around winning medals. I just wanted to do the best gymnastics routines that I could do. I was only 20 years old, but I felt like a really seasoned gymnast. For the six months running up to the Rio Olympics I had been competing pretty much non-stop around the world and performing excellently. I was extremely comfortable with where I was at and what I could do. Performing a gymnastics routine is very much a process, just a series of skills you need to complete, and I felt rock solid in doing that. So that's how it was for me at Rio – I just wanted to perform at my best without any real thought about where that would take me.

We narrowly missed out on a medal in the team event, which was pretty crushing at the time, and a lot of attention was put on Louis Smith's fall from the Pommel Horse for our final score. Much of the media back home blamed Louis for us missing out on a bronze and it was pretty brutal for him on social media. That was really unfair and not the reason we missed out on a medal. Louis had to go for broke in his routine because as a team we had under-performed before him and left him too much to do. When you attempt a routine of the highest difficulty then the margin for error is so small. The slating Louis got was unfair and from people who didn't really understand gymnastics very well. I put in another solid performance in the Individual All-Around final scoring 89.565 and finished eighth. The standard was incredibly high, as you would expect in an Olympics, but for me, I was excelling in my routines. At the biggest event in the sporting world and under the highest pressure, I was performing again and again.

All that was left for me after the Individual All-Around final was the High Bar final which was six days later. Up to that point, I had performed eighteen routines in less than a week. It doesn't matter how strong and fit you are, that is exhausting. It's not just the physical exertion but also the emotions that go through your mind at the time. It was virtually impossible to sleep well after competing with that amount of adrenaline still flowing. Nonetheless, you get into a routine and just keep going. The challenge now was that I had six days where my body and mind would unwind a little. It meant that waiting for my High Bar final was so tough. I was exhausted and just wanted it now but could do nothing but wait. It was probably the only time that my mind wandered to considering whether I would win a medal.

I think it was because I had qualified second for the final and knew I had a decent chance. But every time those thoughts came, I blocked them out and just concentrated on the process I was in. To begin with that was about recovering and preparing during this six-day wait. I perform with a lot of passion and when I roar after sticking a landing people might see me as being an emotional athlete, but the truth is that I am very process-driven gymnast. The build-up, the performance and then the recovery are all dominated by process.

Finally, the day arrived.

I actually slept well the night before as I was in such a good routine, but as soon as I awoke I had the building of a feeling that I had not experienced before. It was like my body knew what was coming and was primed with the adrenaline! I had the usual dull butterflies, but this was a bit different – it seemed as if the intensity that Louis had described to me about the Olympics was starting to build. I travelled easily on the bus to the arena and had my tunes on in my ears. I knew I was ready for this.

I had had some injuries in the build-up to the Olympics – nothing out of the ordinary – my body was in good shape. The consistency of my performances had been so good, and I had done the routine I needed to do that day a million times. Maybe most importantly, I had shown time and time again that on the big stage, I could do it. It didn't faze me. In fact, I loved it. This was my time to make a mark at an Olympics Games.

When I arrived for the warmups in the back hall of the arena, I got to see all the other athletes and coaches. The finalists were Fabian Hambüchen from Germany; Oleg Verniaiev from the Ukraine; Danell Leyva from the US; Sam Mikulak also from the US; Francisco Barreto Júnior from Brazil; Epke Zonderland from the Netherlands; Manrique Larduet from Cuba; and finally, me from Pudsey, Leeds. This was the best of the best at the biggest event imaginable. The whole world stopped to watch the Olympics and we had built ourselves for this very moment. There was such a difference as to how people handled this moment: some were smiley and engaging; others had their heads down and didn't want any sort of interaction with anyone else. I was definitely the former, but I don't think I had ever felt so present at any moment in my life. The intensity that Louis described was just getting stronger and stronger. People have asked me to try and compare this with other sporting moments, but I am not sure I can really. We don't play an eighty- or ninety-minutes match in which lots of different things can happen, we have one sixty or so seconds routine that everything rests on – just one go. And that routine involves us swinging around a bar at high pace and then letting go and catching it multiples times while twisting and changing our hand positions. The risk level is extremely high. Add to this that we are acutely aware that the next time we might get this opportunity is in four years' time, not next week. So, how do you compare this with any other sporting moment? I don't think you can.

I had my three minutes on the bar as my warmup and felt good; there was nothing more for me to really do. 'I can do this', I kept telling myself. I had done so much work over the last four years with my mentor Michael Finnigan around my self-talk and the positive affirmations were just conditioned in. But it wasn't just me telling myself that in some sort of con against lingering doubts in my mind, I truly believed it – I had truly done this a million times.

Back in January 2016, Michael Finnigan and I had sat down, and I had written my 'Inevitable Dream'. It read: 'Last man up on the High Bar. I perform a spotless routine and stick the dismount. Soak up the roar of the crowd and slowly lift my head and start laughing … then I win the crowd.'

From that moment to the Olympic High Bar final, I had practised this exact scenario millions of times. Yes, in training but also in my head. I would stand in the shower and visualise every part of my Inevitable Dream. I would do it again and again. There wasn't a day that went by in which I hadn't visualised that exact scenario.

The intensity of the Olympic final was nearly at a crescendo now. For all eight of us, this was our moment to be part of Olympic history. As we walked into the arena in front of 20,000 people, I immediately could see where Mum, Dad and Joanna were in the crowd. That was important to me – I loved being able to know where they were, partly so I knew where to celebrate when I stuck my landing! 'I can do this', I kept saying to myself. There were no inspirational words needed now from a coach, I was entirely in the moment of what I needed to do.

Fabian Hambüchen went first and absolutely nailed it his routine with a brilliant score of 15.766. What a high-quality start to the final!

It was now Epke Zonderland's turn. Epke was the reigning Olympic High Bar Champion with a huge reputation. Incredibly, he fell off the bar! From the utter brilliance of Fabian to the massive mistake of Epke, it could not have been a more different start to the competition.

I was third up.

As I chalked up my hands and walked to the bars, time stood still. That moment of intensity that Louis had told me about so long ago was here in full force. It truly was indescribable. The truth is that Fabian's routine and Epke's mistake had made no difference to me. This was about me, not them or anyone else in the final. This was about me performing my best gymnastics. This was about me doing a High Bar routine that I had done a million times before one more time. Just before my coach lifted me on to the bars, I shouted one more time 'I can do this!'

I know my family would have been shouting but I could hear nothing. My mind and body were so present in what I needed to do, everything else was irrelevant. 'I can do this'.

I don't remember my routine. I don't remember performing my first skill, a Cassina, and I don't remember going through any of the other skills. I don't remember feeling anything.

It was like muscle memory on the most extreme steroids imaginable. It was a blur. All the times I had visualised and practised this exact moment seemed to connect with my mind and body so that it knew

exactly what it was doing – I was on autopilot. And then suddenly …
I was preparing for my release, I let go, I was in the air and my feet
hit the ground. I stuck it. I stuck the dismount! As I straightened
my legs, I felt this surge of emotion through my body as I screamed
out loud and started laughing. The crowd roared and I looked to my
family who were going nuts! I had nailed it – 15.466.

My Inevitable Dream had just happened.

I walked back to the gymnasts' waiting area and as I gathered
my thoughts, it suddenly dawned on me that I had 'done it'. I had
been telling myself again and again that I could do it but then in the
most intense moment, I had actually done it. There was joy but also
massive relief. What you tell yourself in your head has huge meaning
and power, but then to have actual proof of it was mind blowing. In
an Olympic final, I had done my best gymnastics. Looking back, it
wasn't absolutely perfect, but it was a damn good clean routine.

The one thing that I hadn't prepared for now happened: I had to
wait. In all my preparation, I had never contemplated that I would
be in silver medal position and having to wait for five other gymnasts
to perform. It was pretty unbearable. I watched and waited. One by
one, the first four went up, performed and came back, and I was still
placed in silver medal. With only Danell Leyva left to go, it was real
– I was going to win an Olympic medal. The emotion started to come,
and I struggled to hold back the tears. Everything I had dreamt and
hoped for was here with me now; I was making history – this was
Great Britain's first ever Olympic medal in the High Bar.

Danell was excellent and nudged me into bronze but it didn't take
anything away from the moment. I looked up at my family and the
emotions were just overwhelming for them and for me. I hugged
people, I'm not even sure who, and did some sort of interview that
I can't even remember! It was just another blur as we quickly got
ready for the medal ceremony. There was no real time to take stock of
what had just happened.

I had done it.

I went to the back changing areas and got changed into my Team GB tracksuit as the medal ceremony was no more than ten minutes after Danell had finished his routine. As I walked back towards the arena, our team physiotherapist handed me a mobile phone and it was one of my coaches, Baz Collie. He could hardly speak. He was crying, shouting and completely overwhelmed with emotion. We barely got a word out between us, but it was an amazing moment. I had been through so much with Baz and he had pushed and inspired me in so many ways over the years. He was, and still is, a brilliant person in my life. He had seen me grow as an athlete and as a person, so this moment was huge for him. Just that simple blabbering exchange on the phone seconds before the medal ceremony was enough for us to recognise how much this meant.

As I walked to the podium and then stepped up to receive my medal, the emotion was too much. I cried with a mixture of pure joy, relief and exhaustion. I looked at my family and saw how much it meant to them as well. All those years of hard work and dedication from all of us came to fruition right then and there. From my mum taxiing me back and forth from training, to my dad working his backside off to support my dreams and to Joanna waiting at training for me to finish night after night – we had all given so much to this. Yes, my medal was for me, but it was for all of us.

I had dreamt this moment a million times and it was more special than I could ever imagine.

Chapter 4

Post Rio

It is fair to say that everything after the medal ceremony was one long party!

All the athletes and their families were able to go to the Team GB House, a big party building in the middle of Rio, for free drinks and food. It was a pretty spectacular spot, with a view of the famous 'Christ the Redeemer' statue through the roof. I had to do a drugs test after the medal ceremony, so my family went ahead to the Team GB House. I still hadn't been able to see them at this point.

When I finally arrived and got out of the taxi, my mum, dad and sister were all waiting for me. We had this massive embrace that I will never forget. There was just pure joy as we were all trying to get our heads around what had just happened. My dad shook me by the shoulders and said 'Son … you did it' as we cried and laughed. It was an incredible mixture of disbelief and elation; everyone just trying to take stock of the moment. And that's when the celebrations began! Being able to celebrate something so huge with my family was one of the most special moments of my life. The venue was incredible with all these amazing people walking around; my dad managed to pin Steve Redgrave down for a half-hour chat – something he will never forget. In the end, Joanna and I went off to an after-party that Louis had got us in to in this huge mansion, which was insane. It was going to be a long night, but there was no chance I would be able to sleep. Later, Louis and I walked into the Olympic Village at 6.15 a.m. and straight to the food hall for pizza! As I drunkenly munched away at my food, I suddenly realised I had to do a full day of media in about an hour's time!

I rushed back to the apartment for a shower, changed into my Team GB tracksuit and guzzled a pint of water. The truth is that I was still pretty tipsy so felt OK about everything. Before I knew it, I was live on *Sky News* doing my absolute best not to slur my words! The rest of the day became gradually more difficult as my hangover kicked in. I eventually got back to the apartment at 3 p.m. for a couple of hours' sleep before starting the party all over again! We had six days in Rio after my Olympic final and it just became a lads' holiday.

The journey home was crazy. We flew with British Airways and the medal winners were given upgrades – gold medallists were in First Class, silver medallists were in Business Class and bronze medallists were in Premium Economy. There weren't actually that many bronze medallists but there was a good number of gold medallists because the women's hockey team had won gold! So the hockey players were all moved to Premium Economy with me. By this point, I had barely slept for six days and was completely exhausted, but the hockey girls were still flying high. A video went viral on social media of the girls dancing and singing the National Anthem at the top of their voices while I was in the background fast asleep in my seat! As soon as I was back in Leeds, it was straight to Leeds Gymnastics Club for a celebration, which seems pretty ironic after how things have played out with them over the last couple of years.

I guess the question now was how do you come down from something as big as you fulfilling a lifelong dream?

The simple answer is that I didn't want to find out. I just wanted to stay up on cloud nine and not come down.

This sounds fun and don't get me wrong, it really was, but the next twelve weeks were a write-off for me. I was suddenly famous. Every bar and nightclub in Leeds let me in for free and I didn't have to pay for a drink. People swamped me for photos and there was constant attention. Looking back, I had had this enormous hit of dopamine in my body that created this hugely intense experience and a high that is indescribable. I was out on the town at least four nights a week partying with my mates. I just couldn't face coming back down to reality. I didn't want it to end. Was this a sign of some of the problems I was to face in the next four years around not coping with reality? Yeah, probably.

Eventually, my constant partying could not be excused by my coaches and family any longer. My 'Olympic celebrations' were now way beyond anything normal. I was meant to go to a couple of World Cup events that I had agreed to before the Olympics, but I was withdrawn from them because I was in no shape to compete. I was made to sit down, was told enough was enough and I needed to get back into the gym. That intervention and, in truth, my vanity over the weight I was putting on, did drag me back into the gym, but the training was nothing high end. I found it incredibly hard to get back into life after the Olympics. I don't know how it is for every Olympian but for me, it was a real struggle. I remember sitting in my kitchen with Mum going through a list of chores I needed to do, yet only a few weeks previously I had been experiencing the most intense emotions possible. I didn't know what to do with myself. Adam Peaty has described it as the 'Olympic Blues' and for me it was really strong. I would find myself staring at my medal and crying my eyes out. I didn't know where to go from there. Having experienced such a high, I didn't really want real life any more. Everything just felt so out of place. These were warning signs for me; I just didn't know it at the time.

The one thing that did help me focus during the winter of 2016 and then 2017 was YouTube. I really got involved in producing content and I was uploading a lot of videos. I was loving it and it helped give me some focus back again. As we rolled into 2017, both my YouTube and my body were about to have a massive shock.

It was the weekend of my twenty-first birthday and Jay Thompson and Bryn Evans came to stay at my house for the party. As we were having breakfast that morning, I suggested to the lads that we go into the gym and film some stuff for YouTube. I came up with the concept of the 'Ultimate Gymnastics Challenge' where we would compete against each other in a series of physical challenges. They agreed and it was brilliant. My twenty-first celebrations then took place, and it was an incredible weekend of fun. The video with Jay and Bryn waited for me to edit and release it.

That next week, I was in the gym and again videoing myself for YouTube when I landed badly off the Parallel Bars. I heard a snap and immediately knew something was very wrong – the pain was agonising. I had snapped my ankle ligaments. All of this was caught on camera because I had left it running while I trained. The scans revealed I needed surgery and would be facing a six to seven months' rehabilitation period. It was really bad news after the huge success at the Olympics. As if the injury wasn't bad enough, the fall-out from it was also damaging. The fact that I had been filming myself while the accident happened didn't go down well with my coaches. It's fair to say that I took a massive bollocking about it as they questioned whether my head had been focused on the filming or my gymnastics. The truth is that it was going to be the first of many times that my vlogging was questioned by my coaches.

As I waited for surgery, I edited and uploaded my Ultimate Gymnastics Challenge video with Jay and Bryn. In the first five days, it got about 10,000 views, which was pretty normal for where I was at during that time. But then on the night before surgery, I looked again, and it was on 40,000 views. I remember thinking 'shit, what has happened here?' This was far more than usual! I went into surgery and when I came round from the general anaesthetic, I checked again – 200,000 views! 'Holy shit!' This was mad. The number of video views was now accelerating rapidly as it was going viral. Within the next week, the video charged towards a million views and my YouTube channel exploded to life. As views went up so did my subscribers – it was as though a rocket had taken off!

The mad thing was that in the matter of a couple of weeks, I had suffered a really bad career injury for my gymnastics, but at virtually the same time I had also had a huge boost to my career away from gymnastics. The next few weeks and months were tough for me as the rehabilitation from my ankle injury was really slow, but I just threw myself into my YouTube channel. I decided to document my whole journey of recovery from my injury, and the Ultimate Gymnastics Challenge video had given me this influx of new audience. My engagement levels were just off the charts and I started to see how I could make some serious money via YouTube. I had been producing videos since I was 14 and I felt as though I had developed a really strong feel for what made for interesting content. I wanted to inspire people, but also make them laugh. Gymnastics is an incredible sport to watch, but I knew my content could be much more than just about the sport.

On a business front, 2017 was a life-changing year for me. My YouTube channel was able to generate such a massive amount of traffic that my businesses 'Body Bible', gymnastics-based training programmes; and 'NW Clothing', my own merchandise range, just exploded. Luke Sutton became my manager in March of that year as well and we immediately had this brilliant chemistry between us. Up and until the start of 2017, the most I had earned was around £35,000 in a year. A big chunk of that was from my UK Sport funding and the rest was from sponsorship and appearances. Suddenly, I was in a position where I could be earning as much as five times that amount. This is not unheard of in gymnastics – Louis was definitely able to earn that sort of money in the run-up to London 2012 and Max had probably done very well; the key difference was that I was generating this sort of income a year after the Olympics when incomes normally slow down significantly for athletes. I was also injured so my earnings were not coming from stellar competition performances. This community of the best and most loyal fans, The Wilsonators, was growing all the time and from all over the world.

Despite all this, my injury did mean I soon slipped into bad habits with partying. I didn't need to be in the gym six hours a day and six days a week; I had the freedom to go out more. Every weekend became a big weekend of drinking and those weekends would become longer than they should be. As had happened previously, it eventually got to the place where people intervened. When I was in this pattern, I found it so difficult to extract myself from it and it would need the intervention of my coaches, or my family, or Luke. The World Championships were in Montreal, Canada, at the start of October and I did have a chance of making them, but I needed everything to go right with my ankle. While I was in my partying cycle, I was making the chances of this less and less. In July, after a talking to, I stopped myself from going out that weekend. That one weekend meant that I went into the next week fresh and had a brilliant week of training. Suddenly that was it – I switched the pattern into the total opposite. I dedicated myself to my training and stopped drinking entirely. It was that all-or-nothing mentality with me and now I was back in the zone. My ankle injury meant that I was racing against time to be fit for Montreal, but I loved that sort of challenge. To begin with, I needed to qualify for the World Championships, and I knew there were a few people wondering whether I would be in good enough shape to do that. I knew I could be and, more importantly, I knew that when it came to the moment to perform, I always had it in me. Sure enough, I won the qualifying event for the All-Around in September. I was going to Montreal.

Considering I had been injured for vast majority of the year, what I achieved in Montreal was actually really special. I came sixth in the All-Around against the very best gymnasts in the world, when only a couple of months previously I was still having to be careful how much load I put through my ankle in training. I surprised a lot of people and even though I hadn't won a medal, I gained a massive amount of confidence from it. Even without enough preparation time, I was still right up there with the world's best. The other incredible thing I saw in Canada was people walking around the arena wearing my 'Train Smart, Keep It Real' T-shirts and hoodies. I was thousands of miles away from Leeds and there were proud Wilsonators coming to support me in my merchandise – it blew my mind!

After such a tough start to 2017, I went into the end of the year feeling so happy. I was training well, with my injuries mostly under control and my business interests outside of gymnastics flying. In a single year, my YouTube subscribers had increased from around 15,000 to over 600,000. I was one of the fastest-growing YouTubers in the UK that year. We were now in the two-year run-in to the Tokyo Olympics and things were coming together nicely for me. To add to this, the next major competition for me was the Commonwealth Games in the Gold Coast, Australia. I loved the Commonwealth Games because it represented that first incredible experience I had at a senior level in 2014 in Glasgow. As the New Year ticked over to 2018, I felt so excited about what was to come.

I had suffered with a wrist injury for years, dating back to the 2014 World Championships in China. It was a chronic pain through my right wrist and hand that could flare up badly when I was on the Pommel Horse. I had numerous cortisone and pain-killing injections in it which helped manage it, but it had never gone away entirely. When it got really bad I had to have some time off the Pommel Horse training, which was never ideal because it was my weakest apparatus. I knew that my flight path to gold at Tokyo was going to involve improving my routine on the Pommel Horse, so I didn't want to lose any more time in training on it due to my wrist. Despite being in decent shape in the first three months of 2018, my wrist was becoming an increasing problem. As the Commonwealth Games qualifying events came along, I knew I had a problem with doing a routine on the Pommel Horse. If I couldn't do this then there was no way I could take part in the All-Around. Despite this doubt, I was selected for the squad knowing that if the worst came to worst, I could still take part in the team event and some individual finals.

It was agreed that I would have another injection in my wrist, and I worked with my coach, Dave Murray, to see if there was a very basic routine that I could do on the Pommel Horse that wouldn't trigger the wrist pain. The main issue for me was going up on the handles during a routine. The position it put my wrist in created incredible pain, but it was a necessity in order to achieve a high score. So we worked on whether there was a way that I could perform a low-scoring routine in the twelves by avoiding the handles that would be enough to keep me in the race for the All-Around gold. As I boarded the plane for Australia, I started to feel this was possible.

In many ways the 2018 Commonwealth Games was my perfect storm. As a gymnast, and despite my wrist injury, I was right on top of my game. I was confident and ready for the competition. Away from the gymnastics, my YouTube channel was exploding. I was enjoying creating content and my channel was fast approaching 1 million subscribers. As I arrived at the Games, I made a decision to go for everything – I was going to win as many medals as I could and put out as much content as I could. Some people might have questioned whether this was all too much for me, but I felt I could do it.

My family travelled out to Australia and when they arrived I told them that I was going to do the All-Around with a basic Pommel Horse routine. We had all thought that this wasn't going to be possible, but now that it was, it created this amazing buzz about what was to come. Could I pull this off and win gold?

The competition was an absolute dream – I smashed it! Even with my low-scoring Pommel Horse routine (12.60), I was left with a High Bar routine to win the gold medal in the All-Around and nailed it with a score of 15.10! We won the team gold, and I won another gold in the High Bar; and picked up two silver medals on the Rings and Parallel Bars. It was incredible and my three golds and two silvers made me England's most successful gymnast ever at a Commonwealth Games.

Away from the gymnastics, I released seven YouTube videos during the Games, which I had edited entirely myself. All the videos went mad with engagement and were a massive success – although I did manage to accidentally tell the world what Tom Daley's mobile number was during one of them! His phone was ringing non-stop for twenty-four hours. Oops! It was just a brilliant Games for me in every way and with the clock ticking down to the 2020 Tokyo Olympics, everything was looking good. My wrist injury was a concern, but everyone hoped that with some rest after the Games, it would settle back down again. It was only April and I had the European Championships in Glasgow in August and the World Championships in Doha at the end of October still to come. I was confident about what I could do at both of those events and felt as though 2018 could be a big year of medals for me.

Unfortunately, little were we to know but the 2018 Commonwealth Games was probably the beginning of the end for me.

Chapter 5

Commonwealth Games Come-Down

Looking back now, I realise that the demands I had placed on myself at the Commonwealth Games with my gymnastics performance and my YouTube content were not sustainable. Doing either thing on its own was a huge effort but doing them together just took too much out of me. It wasn't as though I was competing in one or two events or just trying to push out one or two videos during the Games – this was an extreme effort and although I had really good outcomes, it took a massive amount out of me. Post Games, it wasn't that surprising that I suffered a similar crash to after the Olympics.

I was exhausted. I needed a break but had just set myself this crazy standard – demanding so much of myself in all areas of my life and all at once. I found it difficult to get back into training and that is when the drinking started again. I struggle with balance my life; I am extreme in everything I do and eventually it takes its toll. When I am pushing to the extreme, I am at my best but there comes a point where my body and mind say 'stop'. It was a massive challenge for me to get back into a decent routine in May 2018.

By June, I had got myself back into training pretty well, but it was the first time that I felt my neck pain. I was doing a front uprise, double back on the Parallel Bars and as I hit the bottom of the swing, I felt this pain through my neck. It was immediately pretty painful and I couldn't train at all for two weeks while we waited for it to settle down. I was in a familiar position of having a race against time to be fit for a major event – this time it was the European Championships in August. What everyone has to remember is that the squad can't carry serious injury risks. You can't bring in a replacement the night before or during the competition, so if you are a big part of the team's performance, as I was, then doubt on whether I could compete was often too big to justify a place in the team. As I raced to be fit for August, the neck never properly settled. It would seem as though it had, yet every time we had to increase the training load on it, it flared up badly again and I would have to ease off. In the end, it was decided that I wouldn't go to the Europeans and would have an epidural injection in my neck. This would ease the pain and inflammation and I would now have more time to be ready for the World Championships at the end of October.

The epidural actually worked brilliantly and for six months my neck felt great. Ahead of the Worlds, I trained well and felt I was ready to pick up where I had left off after the Commonwealth Games. But on the Friday before we were due to leave for Doha on the Monday, when I was doing a controlled competition with the rest of the Great Britain squad, I had a freak injury. As I practised on the Parallel Bars, I caught my finger on the way through and snapped a ligament in my middle finger. It was bad, but I desperately wanted to find a way to still go to the Worlds. There was a possibility that my finger would settle down to some extent or I could I have another pain-killing injection that would still allow me to compete – I was hanging on to those possibilities. It was less than twenty-four hours to the flight to Doha and my packed bags were waiting in the hallway as I went from phone call to phone call between Paul Hall, Baz Collie, Dave Murray, my family and Luke. There was a chance that my finger might hold up, but there was also a big chance it wouldn't. It all went back to whether the team was able to carry my risk and, in the end, it couldn't.

I understood, but I was absolutely devastated.

I had been injured before and had missed competitions before, but missing the Europeans and now the Worlds in the same year hit me really hard. After the massive high of the Commonwealth Games in April, it felt as though I couldn't catch a break. I couldn't get into a rhythm with my training as my fitness became an issue all the time. With the countdown to the Tokyo Olympics, these were not competitions I wanted to miss. Since returning from the 2016 Rio Olympics, my time injured far outweighed my time being fit.

I had lived all my life to be an elite gymnast, but I didn't feel I was one right there and then. My body wasn't up to it and I felt this immediate sense of loss. As I had done previously, I just didn't want to deal with the pain and disappointment I felt. I wanted an 'out'. This was generally alcohol, but in the past had also been gambling. This time around, it was focused on gambling. I remember feeling so low and one of my best mates, Luke Stoney, called me and asked me to come and watch him and some other lads play 5-a-side football, rather than sit on my own in my apartment. I had a beer in the bar while they played just around the corner from the casinos. I just felt useless. The other lads in the Great Britain squad were boarding their flight to go to Qatar and here I was with a mashed finger, drinking a beer.

On the way home, I knew I shouldn't turn into the casinos. I knew the issues I had with gambling and once I opened that tap, it was very difficult to turn off. I knew all of this.

'Don't do it', I said again and again to myself. But I didn't listen.

I just wanted a distraction from the way I was feeling about myself and life. Not knowing how to sit and deal with that pain, I just walked straight back into my old self-destructive pattern of behaviour. My 'excuse' was that I only had thirty or forty minutes to spare because I was meeting my then girlfriend afterwards – 'what real harm could I do?' is what I told myself as I walked into the casino.

The truth is that in that time I did a lot of harm. In fact, the worst thing happened – I won. I won £1,000 in half an hour then had to leave. I felt this rush and buzz that gave me exactly what I wanted. It distracted me from how fed up I was feeling about life and the win confirmed in my misplaced thinking that there were positives to come from this. I had taken thirty minutes out of my day to make myself feel better and I had won £1,000, how could that be that bad?

These were all the same things that I had told myself when I was 19 years old and had got myself into difficulties with gambling previously. But deep down I knew the truth. That's why I didn't call my family or Luke to tell him what had happened. It was now a secret that was buzzing around in my head. The tap had been opened and I knew it meant trouble.

From October to Christmas 2018, my gambling just escalated. It was just like my previous issues with it, but this time my financial situation had changed significantly. I had access to much more money. I was winning big and losing bigger, even if I didn't want to admit that to myself. I would take the cash from my casino winnings home with me and store it in my apartment, and when I returned to the casino, I would use my bank card again. At one point, I had £11,000 in cash stored at my apartment. It was crazy but maybe it was some way of convincing myself that I was 'saving' money because I could see it. It was all part of the insanity of these vicious cycles. Luke and I have a different set up now for my finances but back then I could access my savings whenever I wanted, which wasn't a good thing at all.

The strongest part of it all, though, was that gambling was consuming so many of my daily thoughts. This was a period that I needed to get back into a decent training routine, but my mind was never far away from wondering when I could next go back to the casino. It just gripped me so comprehensively and yet I was still keeping it mainly a secret. My best mates, Luke Stoney and Ash Watson, knew about it and I started to open up to Luke about it, but I never told him the full extent of it. I think Luke could always tell because there would be a significant shift in my behaviour. I became less interested in business and harder to get hold of, and everything was greyer for me. I would lose enthusiasm in new ideas and my normal creative mind would just become a bit stuck.

If I put it all into perspective now, it's crazy to think how far off my bearings I became. At that time, I was still a serious medal contender for the 2020 Tokyo Olympics with just under two years to go to the

Games. My neck injury was under control at this time and my finger injury was nothing too significant, even though it had forced me to miss the Worlds. Outside of the gym, my businesses were doing well and financially I was secure. And yet, despite all this, I had just fallen off the edge of a cliff due to missing a major championship. It was as though I had no capacity to cope with that setback.

As Christmas approached, I couldn't escape the fact that my gambling was in a really bad place. I needed to find a way to get out of the hole I was in and spoke more and more to Luke Stoney about it.

'You know what you need to do mate,' he said one day.

With that, we went to the casino together. I took £2,500 from my cash reserves at the apartment with me. It was gone within twenty minutes of arriving at the casino – I had lost the lot. So, I went to the cash point and withdrew the maximum I could on my daily allowance. Another twenty minutes and that was all lost as well. It was hideous.

Luke said to me again, 'You know what you need to do mate.'

I walked over to the casino manager and asked to speak to him.

'Please can I ban myself from the casino?'

He immediately said that was possible, but asked if I just wanted to be banned from this casino or all casinos in the UK. Initially, I just said that casino, but then Luke gave me a bit of a sideways glance and I realised how ridiculous that sounded. It would make absolutely no difference to me to just go to another casino in Leeds and carry on what I was doing!

'Please ban me from all casinos in the UK.'

It was done.

It wasn't the entire answer to this problem, but it was a really big step forward. I had found a way out of the cycle I was stuck in. It gave me space to breath and focus my mind fully back on my training. I had lost a lot of time during 2017 and 2018 due to injury and I needed to concentrate on my training during 2019 to hit 2020 in the place I needed to be to win medals at Tokyo. All my routines needed to be upgraded in order to win gold in the All-Around at the

Olympics. This was all possible, but it would take time. It would need many hours of repetition during training and then additional hours of repetition while under the pressure and fatigue of competition. To truly 'master' a new routine takes weeks, and I would like to explain this more for young gymnasts out there.

By the time I was 18, I had pretty much learnt every skill there was on every gymnastics apparatus. I was a fast learner and obsessed by what I could do next. This meant that over time, as I learnt new skills and performed them comfortably in competitions, I naturally upgraded each skill as far as I could go. For example, I started with a Kovacs on the High Bar, a double somersault over the bar, but then you can do that in a tuck position and then with a full twist, which then eventually upgrades to the Cassina, which is the straight with the full twist that people will see as my first skill within my best routine. However, transferring individual skills into a cleanly executed, ten- or eleven-skill routine while under pressure or tired is a different thing all together. My Great Britain coach, Baz Collie, always explained this process in the best way. These are the steps within Baz's process:

1. Physical Preparation
2. Technical Preparation
3. Skill Acquisition
4. Consolidation
5. Adaptation
6. Success!

Physical preparation is a huge foundation within this process and explains why the lengths of time I was out injured were so disruptive to me improving my routines. You need your body to be strong and fit enough to learn and then master the series of skills you are asking it to do in a routine. Without that physical ability, you are going nowhere. You just can't turn up one day and nail a routine that you have practised on paper. The technical preparation and skill acquisition are very much about identifying which skills and in what order to perform them in, and then practising them repeatedly through hours of training. Putting skills together into a routine is a real art and where brilliant coaches come into their own. There has to be an efficient flow when transferring from one skill to the next in order to keep point deductions to a minimum. Consolidation is the process you go through in truly mastering the routine. This is where you reach the point in training when you can do the routine as if you were riding a bike – almost like doing it on autopilot. This then reaches another level with adaptation. This is where you step away from practising and your body's memory for what is involved in the routine becomes so deeply imbedded that when you step back into the gym for training or competition, it is once again like riding a bike. You can then do this routine when you are fresh or when you are tired and you know it, I mean you really 'know' it! Success is finally achieved when you take this to a competition and deliver a series of skills in a routine that you have done a million times – just like my Olympic final at the 2016 Rio Olympics.

The process I describe above is what I needed, and for that I required uninterrupted time in the gym. That meant injuries had to be at a minimum and I had to have my mind focused on a consistent schedule for my training and recovery. At the back end of 2018 and then the start of 2019, I had wrestled back control on my training and lifestyle, and I started to feel pretty bloody good! With 2019 featuring both European and World Championships again, having missed out on both in 2018, I was hungry to make up for lost time.

With the four-year cycle of Olympic Games, I had lost nearly two years to injury so 2019 was the time when I really needed to begin my serious run-in to Tokyo.

Chapter 6

The Dark of my Neck Injury

I was in Germany with the Great Britain squad in February 2019 for a training camp ahead of the European Championships in April. We were practising routines and my first apparatus was the Parallel Bars, which is obviously one of my strongest. I had been working on a new routine which would genuinely be one of the best in the world. I absolutely nailed it. It was world-class gymnastics and as I landed from the dismount, I knew I was in incredible shape. With European and World Championships to follow that year, I knew I could win gold medals in both. I wasn't alone in thinking that. Teammates and coaches watching thought the same. Having suffered from niggly injuries prior to this, everyone, including myself, thought 'Nile's back'.

My second routine was the Floor. As I worked my way through, I did a tumble, and I felt a sharp pop in my neck. It was too big for me to not notice but I carried on with the routine, finishing with a triple twist. I knew it wasn't right, but it wasn't a 10 out of 10 pain immediately. I'm like any other athlete at that level and will never give in to pain easily. I felt I just needed to carry on and it would be alright.

I went over to Baz Collie and Dave Murray and told them something had happened in my neck, but I carried on to the next apparatus, which was the High Bar. As every minute passed, the pain was getting worse. I put my handguards on and tried a few times on the High Bar, but it was no good at all. I knew there was a problem in my neck now, I just didn't know how big a problem. I went to our team physiotherapist, Johnny, to get it assessed. There was no way that early on they could tell what had happened, but Johnny realised this wasn't just a 'niggle'.

After about an hour, the pain had increased to about 7 out of 10 and it was also transferring down my right arm. My head was racing at a million miles an hour with 'what ifs'. I was at my absolute peak of physical fitness but what now? I had gold medals to win but with every minute the pain was getting worse. It was soon agreed by everyone that it was best that I went home immediately. I could get treatment in Leeds from Gill Davey, my physiotherapist, and the beds in Germany were awful, so no place to sleep with an injured neck! I rang my manager, Luke, and he arranged a flight home as soon as possible. I paid for my and Dave Murray's flight to come home the next day. I was desperate to get back.

That evening the pain got worse and worse. I was in agony by now. The boys were playing on a Play Station and I started to gamble online with roulette. I reckon I played for three to four hours and I was playing with real money. As you know, this wasn't my first time doing this.

Although I managed to get off to sleep it was the worst night's sleep I have ever had; I was in so much pain. When I woke the next morning and got out of bed, the pain was so excruciating, I could barely walk to the bathroom. I hobbled there at snail's pace. What I didn't know was that a disc in my neck was pressing against a nerve, so every step I took brought an explosion of pain. It was absolutely horrific.

It was 7 a.m. and I was not in a good place at all. The team doctor, Chris Thomlinson, was not on the trip, so I begged Johnny for stronger pain killers. He explained that he was not allowed to give them without authorisation from the doctor. It was 6 a.m. in England and I rang the doctor non-stop! Eventually, about an hour later, he picked up and explained that he only had some paracetamol. That was never going to be enough!

Still in agony I managed to get on the flight. It was horrific. Every movement hurt. I just wanted some escape from the pain. Finally, we landed and my girlfriend at the time, Gabs, picked me up from the airport with her sister. They didn't understand the pain I was in and what I was going through mentally, and just dropped me off at my apartment because they had a busy day working. I spoke to Gill and Luke again, and they could hear the pain in my voice. It was excruciating. Gill wanted me to get scanned as soon as possible, which fortunately was to be an hour later. I called an Uber cab to take me to the hospital and started back on the roulette. I played it all the way to and inside the hospital. I could barely listen to the person at reception because all I could now think of was spinning that bloody roulette wheel to see if I would win or not. Was it just my way of distracting my mind from the pain or something a bit deeper? Deep down I knew the truth that when I was this vulnerable, I turned to one of my biggest sins to cope. I reckon I had already lost about £2,000 and I knew I needed to stop. I just had no control over the gambling at this point. It was totally ruling me. I didn't care about anything else in the world, I mean anything else, I just wanted to spin the wheel.

I was in so much pain, the worst pain I had ever felt. Only twenty-four hours earlier I had been doing world-class gymnastics on the Parallel Bars and now I was completely fucked. I could barely walk. With the physical pain, I just couldn't hold it together mentally. After the scan, I rang Chris Thomlison again and begged for some more pain killers. He fortunately got codeine prescribed for me.

When I returned home, I hobbled over to Tesco and bought a bottle of Lanson's Champagne and three bottles of Bulmer's Cider. They were on offer and there was no getting away from them for me. I zeroed in on them.

As I had been decorating my new apartment, I only had a beanbag in the lounge. I settled down, put ice on my neck, started watching a TV series called *The Punisher* and began to drink the booze. I ordered a takeaway and then had a massive fall-out with my girlfriend, who I felt had no understanding of what I was going through. She actually asked me if I was going out that night! I then took three codeine tablets and, all of a sudden, I was completely spaced out. The pain seemed to disappear in a mixture of alcohol, codeine and staying as still as I could. The relief was enormous. It was like heaven to be honest. I was out of the pain I had thought I couldn't escape.

What I didn't realise was that I was starting off a pattern that was to take some serious shifting. Codeine, alcohol and TV. It was all I survived on. Unfortunately, I didn't pay any attention to the fact that I shouldn't be drinking alcohol with codeine, and eventually I got really sick after about a week. I was in and out of gambling, but Luke and I had previously set up a new way for me to draw money out, which involved me having to call him and ask him for more money. I didn't want to have to call him because I was embarrassed, and I knew he would know something was up. It was actually saving me at that time, otherwise I would have been deeper into gambling online as well.

In the brief periods when I wasn't drunk or under the influence of codeine, the pain was still horrific, and it took another two weeks for me to have surgery. Looking back, I realise that I was a mess. Physically I was obviously shot. I actually tried to do a press-up to see how bad it was, and it was shocking. There was nothing in my body. I was trembling and the whole of my right-hand side was powerless. I couldn't do one press-up. I couldn't get a centimetre off the floor and a week or so earlier I had been one of the fittest athletes on the planet. But mentally I was in even worse shape. I wasn't able to cope with what was happening to me, whether it be the pain level or the 'what ifs'. I was just numbing myself with alcohol and codeine. Without realising it, I was falling into a deep hole.

Following surgery and with the pain being somewhat relieved, you would think that I might improve mentally. But I didn't. Not even close. In fact, I fell further. And I didn't know what was wrong with me.

Prior to this time, I didn't believe depression was real. I thought it was a choice. I felt totally lost and I just couldn't shift it. And this wasn't just some days, it was every day. I have had bad days in the past, but I always believed that I could change my thoughts with positive self-talk. Not with this. I couldn't shift it.

The feeling was like an indescribable internal pain that I couldn't get out of. It was suffocating, sick, dark, lost, hopeless, alone, lonely. Lost was the big one for me. No one could see it and it felt as though no one, most importantly me, could fix it. I just wanted out from it. I didn't know if I was suffering from depression, but I knew I was riddled with anxiety. I wouldn't wish it on anyone.

Symptoms such as shortness of breath, achy pain in the stomach and chest. I couldn't do anything about it when it was there. It came and went when it wanted. And if you asked me what was wrong and why I felt that way, I wouldn't be able to tell you. I had anxiety about getting anxiety.

One night I was lying in bed with my girlfriend, Gabs, and everything was good. We were cuddling and she was falling asleep. I finished watching some snooker on my phone and put my head on the pillow, and then bang it was there. Anxiety just engulfed me. I started crying and Gabs woke up and asked me what was wrong. 'I don't know, I don't fucking know.' I was shaking, heavy breathing and crying. I had to go and sit outside on my balcony and I couldn't sleep until 4 a.m.

What added to all of this was how I found ways to cope (or rather not cope!). I just wanted rid of the pain. Numb it or take me away from it. I had physical pain through my neck injury but now it felt like mental torture. I just wanted out.

Short term, drinking was brilliant. My best friend, in truth. In that moment, it took away the anxiety. It felt as though it removed some of my emotions. After five drinks, anxiety had gone, no more dark thoughts. I was rid of the pain. It was a total relief.

Long term, it was the worst thing I could be doing. I wasn't drinking for pleasure and for celebration. I was drinking for self-destruction, until I passed out. It started as pain relief but then it became a matter of me punishing myself because of the way I was living my life. How I felt about myself. I wouldn't just drink five drinks; I would drink a bottle of vodka. I wouldn't go out for a few hours; I would go out for eighteen hours and then wake up and do it again over. A Bank Holiday weekend was a disaster for me. Seventy-two hours of minimal sleep and as much as I could drink.

I am not a nasty drunk or person, but during this time I became different. I would just snap and lose it. I once lost it outside of Fibre nightclub in Leeds. I know the people there well, but I was screaming at the bouncers in front of a huge queue, because they wouldn't let my friends in as they were wearing trainers. I was an embarrassment, but that's where I had got to. I started being nasty to people and even friends. I was just angry and lost. Angry with myself. Looking back, drinking was the worst thing I could have been doing.

There are other examples of how self-destructive I was being.

During one weekend, I had been out with the lads and two girls had come back to my apartment. We were absolutely hammered. One of the girls was a bit overweight. All of a sudden, they got up and left and we didn't know why. A few days later, I was in the gym with the doctor doing some rehabilitation work on my neck when a message popped up in the group WhatsApp chat I had with the lads.

Ashley Watson, an ex-gymnast and one of my best friends, wrote:

'You'll never guess why the girls left …'

'Nile called one of them fat!'

I just froze after reading it. Hearing that about myself, doing that and speaking to someone like that, devastated me. Apparently, I hadn't said it directly to her, but in any case they had heard, and it was terrible and unacceptable. I am not nasty person and would never want to say something like that to anyone, but it just showed the place I was in. I was so drunk; I didn't remember and something like that came out of my mouth. I was angry and lost with the whole situation in my life. I stopped training. I hated myself. I HATED myself.

'I don't deserve to be here. I'm fucking horrible,' I said to myself.

I didn't particularly realise it, but everyone was getting very worried about me, no one more so than my family and my manager. Luke has had his own mental health battles in the past, so he understood, but it was much harder for my family.

I can imagine that when you are parent and your child is in difficulty you want to fix it, but this was something you couldn't put a plaster on. They didn't really understand what to do or say.

I went for a week's training at Lilleshall to be under the supervision of the British Gymnastics medical and coaching team for my rehabilitation programme and actually started to feel I had turned a corner. Luke and I had had some really good conversations and I was going into that weekend knowing I wouldn't drink and, with my rehabilitation, was progressing nicely. Mentally I felt better, although there was still some way to go.

My dad texted me to ask me to go and see him and my mum on the Friday night when I got back. I immediately got anxious as I suspected what the conversation would be about.

I wasn't wrong.

I went round and the conversation got really nasty very quickly. My dad said things to me that could have ruined our relationship forever. I felt as though I'd lost my parents. They didn't get it. They just shouted at me.

They had been watching my drinking and behaviour and were really concerned. I had been making some poor decisions and the only time my parents were seeing me was when I was hungover, not eating and stuck on my phone; so of course, they got worried, angry and frustrated. I can understand that they thought they needed to intervene. But they hadn't seen me during the week or understood what I was battling with. They got it wrong, but they were doing what they thought was right, which is all any parent can do.

Unfortunately, at the time, it was the worst possible thing they could have done. I had stopped drinking but then I felt I had hit rock bottom again immediately after that conversation.

The indescribable pain returned and just suffocated me. I drove back to my apartment and sat in the underground car park in the dark. I just cried for an hour. Deep sobbing. It was one of the times when I ran suicide through my mind. I didn't want to be present. I never got to the point where I said, 'yeah, I am going to do it', but I definitely thought through the scenario. What I mean by that is that I contemplated and definitely understood why people would do it. It was one of the darkest moments of my life.

I couldn't shift the pain and my anxiety was off the scale. My mind was just playing out the whole suicide scenario. Fortunately, one of my best friends, Luke Stoney, was coming over as we were meant to be going out for some food that night. Luke and I started gymnastics together when I was 7 and he was 9 years old and we have been best friends since I was 13. We used to go into town on double dates as teenagers and have always been incredibly close. Luke is one of the kindest and most caring people I know in life. I know that if I called him for help, he would always be there for me regardless of what was going on for him at that time. This moment was no different. He called to check we were still on for going out for food but could hear in my voice that I needed him. He immediately said he would rush around. It forced me to get up and be in my apartment just as he arrived. I couldn't hide how I was feeling, and I told him, which was a godsend. Sharing it was a huge relief. I didn't drink that evening and managed to get through the rest of the weekend without a drink. It scares me to think of people feeling like they can't tell anyone and being lost in those dark thoughts.

I have realised that mental health issues affect everyone around you. I just didn't know what to say or do. I was self-obsessed with my dark thoughts. I also didn't realise how hard it was for everyone around me, most of all my parents. My dad's words to me that night had been nasty and patronising. He was trying to shout me out of the situation, but I needed him to put his arm around me. I felt I had lost my parents because there was so much judgement. They didn't

I started gymnastics at the age of 4 and have been obsessed with the sport ever since!

Me and my baby sis on my first day of High School.

Back when my dad used to have bigger biceps than me. That all changed when I was around 15 years old.

My proudest moment! Olympics bronze medallist.
PA Images/Alamy Stock Photo

Chilling with my sis after winning Commonwealth gold in the Gold Coast.

Posing for the camera during my High Bar dismount at the Rio Olympics.
PA Images/Alamy Stock Photo

Trusting the process and training smart. *British Gymnastics*

I always loved competing at the Commonwealth Games, especially on the High Bar. *PA Images/Alamy Stock Photo*

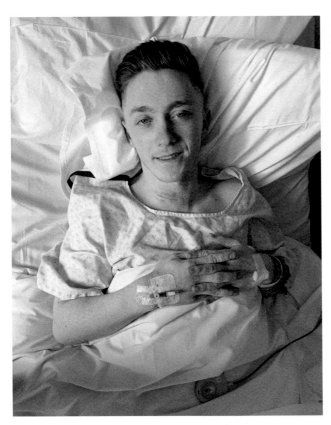

Managing to crack a smile even shortly after major neck surgery.

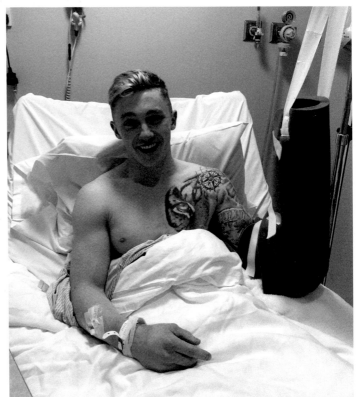

I have had quite a lot of surgeries due to gymnastics injuries, two of which have been on my wrist.

Hitting 1 million subscribers on YouTube. What a moment!

My best friends are cooler and crazier than yours.

YouTube has allowed me to do a lot of awesome collaborations, one of my favourites was with the legendary Ross Edgely.

The Three Musketeers.

I bought my dream apartment in Leeds City Centre when I was 22 years old.

My crazy family are so supportive of everything I do, even when it involves making them do silly things for my vlogs.

ask me if they could help, they just wanted me to snap out of it. My dad is an emotional man and thought that if he told me strongly enough to get out of it, I would. Actually, it was pushing me further down. But all of this was done out of love, confusion and frustration. My parents were brought up in an era when people didn't openly talk about mental health. My dad was told by his dad to stop crying otherwise he'd be given something to cry about!

My dad knows he got things wrong that night. He wanted my behaviour to stop, and quickly. And he wanted to get rid of his own pain, the same as I was doing; to shout at me to fix me but also to fix his own frustration with me. A short-term fix, just as I was using alcohol. But long term, it doesn't work. Actually, it makes everything ten times worse. Now he knows, as I do. I have to understand that as my father he had controlled so much in my life up till then and wanted to do the same with this but didn't know how.

I have learnt a lot from my manager, Luke, about dealing with anxiety. You have to sit with anxiety and own it. Change your relationship with it. You want to get rid of it but to recover from it, you have to sit there with it. Don't try and figure it out, but understand it is real and know it will pass. Don't look for a quick fix. Flip it and sit with it and let it pass like clouds in the sky. Don't hide from it.

When you do that, you feel so empowered. And that happens with all things when you come through the most difficult times. Like the moment with my parents. I didn't blow out after that, I actually sat with it at the worst possible time. That empowered me to know that I could do that, even when it is as bad as that.

It has actually developed the relationship with my family. They know they didn't get it right, but I can understand the position they were in. They had got in a muddle with it. I have realised I was so self-consumed and self-absorbed with my own pain, that I didn't realise I was deeply affecting them as well. My behaviour was difficult for them to understand or handle. As much as I didn't know what to do, they also didn't know what to do with me. They were actually going through the journey with me because they love me. But I didn't see that.

I also realised one other thing from that time.

Through my social media, particularly YouTube, I have been able to amplify my personality enormously. My persona, which is entirely real, is the ultra-positive guy with all the answers. 'Feeling down? No problem, watch a Nile Wilson YouTube video and be inspired.' 'Coming back from adversity? No worries, I can help you with that.' 'Want to get fitter? Not a problem, I have the content for you.' And that really was me, I wasn't faking that. I felt as if I had the answers for everyone.

But I didn't have answers for how *I* was feeling. I couldn't 'self-talk' my way out of this. I was telling everyone that attitude was a choice, but I couldn't live it. I couldn't shake the enormous dark cloud that sat on top of me. So not only did I feel suffocated from depression as it was, but I also felt pressure of having to be the person who could 'snap out of it'. But I just wasn't that person.

I felt I still had to produce content for my audience, even though, at that time, I wasn't the person they thought I was. I didn't know what to do. What did I tell them? I felt like a comedian about to go on stage thinking 'I am not funny, I don't have any jokes, what am I going to say to them?'

I tried to fake it, but that just made it even worse. I hated myself for not being able to live up to that. There was a disconnection between reality and what people thought of me. I was being validated by millions of views and hundreds of thousands of likes and comments. Behind it all, though, I hated myself.

It all added to my isolation and the pressure I felt on my shoulders. I have experienced some of the darkest times in my life, but have come through them. I feel empowered and wiser about mental health. I don't con myself that these problems will never come back, I suspect they will. But the next time, I will be better prepared for them.

I realise now that I don't have the answers to everything. And guess what, that's OK too.

Chapter 7

Fuck It

It was 25 August 2019 and the World Championship trials were two weeks away.

It was a race against time. My neck surgery had only been six months earlier, but it wasn't actually my neck that was the issue. The surgery was successful, and everything had healed well, the race was trying to get my body able to cope with the training load necessary for me to be able to perform six semi-decent routines in order to gain selection for the 2019 World Championships. People who don't know gymnastics well often don't realise that you have to be able to get your body into a physical shape so that in can just cope with what it will be put through as an elite gymnast, never mind the skill of the routines! So coming back from injury is as much about carefully loading up the intensity of training, without pushing the body too much too soon and getting another injury. This was a massive challenge for me. Every time we ramped up the training load, my body barked back, and we had to ease off. This was the race against time we faced.

It was touch and go whether I would be able to make the trials, but in the week building up to the London Open (the first trial), I managed to do six routines on the Tuesday without any major reaction on the day. Unfortunately, when I woke up on the Wednesday there was a problem with my right shoulder. Scarily, it was similar in some ways to my original neck injury – neural pain down my right arm, but reassuringly, it was also different – no pain in my neck. I called my manager, Luke, and we decided not to press the panic button just yet. It could just be a temporary reaction to the workload on the day before and might just settle quickly. We decided to leave it until Thursday morning.

By then it was better although not really great. I went to the gym and tried to go through some basic exercises with my coach, Dave. It wasn't good.

I couldn't even support a handstand. All the strength had gone from my right shoulder and I now knew I had a major problem. There was no way I would make the World Championship trials, which obviously meant goodbye to selection.

I had battled so hard to get back from the neck injury, with so many ups and downs, and right at this last moment, my body couldn't take it. I was devastated.

Not only could my body not take it, my mind couldn't either. I just couldn't handle the pain of the situation. I pressed the 'Fuck It' button. I couldn't sit with the pain and just wanted out. Out of my mind.

I went out on the Friday night with my mates and it was a long night. I got what I wanted; I got off my head.

Friday quickly rolled into Saturday. My sister had managed to get my family and me free hospitality tickets for the Ashes Test at Headingley. I was late. Hungover and still trying to pull myself together from the night before. Trouble with my dad started to bubble straight away.

Dad was already worried about my behaviour at times like this. He didn't like it and wanted me to snap out of it, but he just didn't understand it. I wanted release from the pain and then when it started, I struggled to stop it. He wanted me to have control, but I knew that control had left the building a long time ago. I also knew that my behaviour wasn't good enough.

So the atmosphere was tense to say the least. My dad was also drinking, and we were basically a ticking time bomb. As drinking and tension gathered momentum, we reached a point at the end of the day when things exploded. Dad and I had a massive argument outside. I was letting him down, but he was using language that was hurting me to the core. I guess it showed the extent of his frustration.

If I couldn't take the pain on Friday night, then Saturday was no different. I pressed the 'Fuck It' button again.

I guess to some this might sound fun. It wasn't, it was just self-destructive: me wanting to get out of my head. It was familiar territory, but the most worrying part was I didn't really know when this cycle would end once it had started.

I was on my way into Leeds city centre when Luke called me. He had had a text from my sister about the argument that had happened. He listened and I cried, and he told me he would come and see me the next evening. I knew then that this might just save me from adding a third night to this spiral.

Luke arrived at my apartment the next afternoon and I was in a state. Hungover, tired, mentally beaten, just nowhere really. Luke has had his own issues in the past with mental health and alcohol problems. Genuinely, he was probably the best person in the world I could have seen right at that time.

We talked and Luke shared some of his experiences with me. I connected with it immediately. Luke didn't tell me what to do but did challenge me to have a think about who I truly wanted to be. Not from an achievement point of view but as a person, as a human being. He felt that that had been the biggest shift he had made with himself – when he stopped defining himself by achievements, and instead what type of person he was. Even in my haze, I totally understood this.

We went out for something to eat and I guess it saved me from another night of self-destruction.

The day or two after I had seen Luke, my mind was racing. I replayed our conversation over and over again,

Who am I?
A gymnast, a YouTuber, an influencer, a businessman?
A Jack-the-lad, a good son, a good human being?
What am I defined by?

It all felt within touching distance but also so far away. I have always had a side to me that recognised the importance of enjoying the journey of life without being hung up on outcomes. I used to say it over and over again on my YouTube channel for fuck's sake! But I felt as though I'd lost my way. Disconnected. Disconnected from myself, my values, who and what I was – I wasn't sure. Just disconnected. How had that happened?

The back end of 2018 and all of 2019 were desperately hard times for me. I felt lost, without a purpose or a direction. My injuries, mainly my neck, but also my wrist, finger and shoulder, meant I had barely strung two months of top-level gymnastics together at any time.

I had never before realised how much I was defined by my physical abilities within a gym. I had lost them, or they were at least much depleted, and it felt as if I had lost my whole identity at the same time. I couldn't really remember what made me happy any more. I just found myself constantly searching – without being sure what I was searching for – certainly purpose, most definitely happiness, but most of all, I was searching for some meaning in my life. I dipped between periods of feeling good and other times of battling with terrible anxiety.

Up to this point in my life, everything had seemed pretty simple. I lived and breathed gymnastics. YouTube eventually flowed alongside this, as did all the other business things that came along with my success. It had always felt obvious what I needed to do in life: train hard, think big and everything followed from there.

Nothing felt simple now. It was like fog had descended on me and all because I couldn't do what I normally did in the gym. I had always described my head and body in separate terms, with sayings like 'mind over matter', but at this time, I was learning that it was all one. My body wasn't at its best and so my mind wasn't either. I just felt lost.

During this same month I invited my good friend, Ross Edgeley, as a guest on the podcast I had with my dad. Ross is an amazing guy. He had recently completed his world record swim around the whole of Great Britain in 157 days. I have known Ross for a number of years and as much as I have admired him as an athlete, it doesn't compare to how much I have admired him as human being. His outlook on life and challenges was nothing but totally inspiring. The 'Great British Swim' had really raised his profile and he was now getting the airtime he had always deserved. As expected, he was a brilliant guest on the Neil and Nile podcast.

He told us about the Japanese phrase 'ikigai'. A human being's ikigai is essentially their reason to get up in the morning. It is their purpose in life that connects across four key areas: 'That which you love', 'That which the world needs', 'That which you can be paid for' and 'That which you are good at'. Ross explained how as humans we wouldn't ever feel fully satisfied with our work or endeavours unless we were fulfilling our ikigai. And your ikigai would be entirely personal to you. He gave the example that an athlete might go and win an Olympic gold medal, but unless that was their ikigai then even that wouldn't give them a true sense of fulfilment. Ross described how every human should search and then fulfil their ikigai, whatever it was. He had found his in extreme physical challenges, particularly in swimming, and had therefore found his true purpose in life. It was inspiring to hear.

Ross has an incredible ability to make something sound inspiring yet absolutely achievable for anyone. I understood exactly what he was saying, but rather than give me answers, it made me question everything.

Gymnastics had been my world since the age of 4 and everything had always flowed from it. If I was good in the gym, then everything else was good. I was so confused.

Ross's words sounded so beautifully simple, but they raised so many questions for me as they rang loudly in my ears. What was my purpose? What was my ikigai? Why did I feel so lost right now?

Did I feel lost because I was injured or because gymnastics wasn't really my ikigai?

> Did I define myself by gymnastics performance so without it,
> I was nothing? If that was the case, then who the fuck was I?

I wouldn't describe this as mental torture but with less than twelve months to the Olympic Games, I was questioning my very essence for happiness and meaning in my life. It felt a really big deal.

Throughout this period there was no doubt that the environment I had around me was both good and bad and both helpful and not helpful. Some of it my doing and some of it not.

Sporting governing bodies, particularly Olympic ones, are always under enormous pressure to deliver medals. British Gymnastics was no different. Olympic medals meant funding and secured the next four years for the sport. Gymnastics had achieved so much success since Louis Smith's game-changing bronze medal at the Beijing Olympics in 2008. More medals and more money for the sport had flowed. They were glory years!

But with Tokyo 2020 approaching, an Olympic medal already under my belt and with few genuine medal possibilities amongst the GB squad, the pressure to get me right both physically and mentally was mounting. Pressure started from the very top of the organisation and then fed down through every coaching and athlete support level and then eventually to the athlete. In this case, me.

As I kept getting injured, questions were constantly asked about me. Why was I getting injured? Why was I not recovering from my injuries? The blame game started.

I wasn't a robot of an athlete. I had other things in my life. Max Whitlock, a teammate, friend and Olympic gold medallist was basically the total opposite of me. Max kept life very simple, with little else in it other than gymnastics and his family. I respected him so much for that, but it wasn't me. Whether it was YouTube, social media or business, I needed and loved other things in my life. But this approach was always going to be a stick to beat me with when everything wasn't 'perfect'. However, another stick to beat me with was my lifestyle; it wasn't always 10 out of 10 and that was my doing. Whether it affected my recovery from injuries, we will never know, but it was used to criticise me at times. Throughout this period, I felt the pressure of these continuous appraisals of my situation. I understood why they had to happen, and I understood why I presented a unique challenge for British Gymnastics, but I didn't always accept that some of the conclusions were fair.

It was during this period that I started to question my genuine love of gymnastics. I have always been such an open person, so it wasn't a secret. British Gymnastics were aware of my difficulties with my mental health and the medical staff there were incredible in their support of me. Everyone was aware of all this and, I guess, everyone was worried on some level whether I would get to the Tokyo Olympics.

I felt that pressure. I think it comes with being an Olympic athlete. You have this four-year cycle and everything in your life is geared towards the next Olympics. This includes the people around you, first and foremost your family. They live and breathe every step of your Olympic dream and want it so badly for you. My family has always been my greatest source of inspiration and support. Put simply, my mum, dad and sister are incredible people. For them to watch me being so lost with my life and gymnastics in this run-in to the Olympics was tough for them. They so wanted me to win Olympic gold; when my actions didn't align with this they obviously got upset. Dad and I particularly clashed a few times because I seemed so different from the son who approached the previous Olympics. He couldn't understand what I was feeling inside and often reacted emotionally – which ended in a pretty bad result between us.

This sort of pressure also applies to an athlete commercially. Any Olympian will tell you that years two and three of an Olympic cycle can be pretty barren from a commercial earnings point of view. The Olympics are crucial to an athlete's overall earnings. I have worked hard on creating fairly permanent income streams, but still the Olympics mean so much in every way. Less than a year out from

Tokyo, there seemed to be so many big unknowns in my life. I just wanted to feel happy.

My manager, Luke, is more of a big brother to me than anything and he always said to me that through this period I would learn and grow from it. I actually always felt that too. I just wanted to feel some peace with everything sooner rather than later. Pressure was definitely taking its toll on me and it would show itself in horrible, suffocating anxiety.

However, even in the early stages of this period, I did start to realise a couple of really important things.

I wanted my life to be defined by more than just popularity through gymnastics. It was really important to me what sort of person I was. I wanted to be a good son, brother, boyfriend and friend. I wanted to be proud of myself from that point of view. I guess this would seem quite obvious to some people, but my whole life to this point had been defined by my success within gymnastics. This was never greater than at major gymnastics events, but even my rise on YouTube was rooted to my performances as an athlete. The 'Ultimate Gymnastics Challenges' videos I launched on my YouTube channel, which took me to a new level, were me going head-to-head with other people in a series of physical challenges. Everything I did was linked to my performance in the gym. I realised that without it, I was totally lost. But I wanted there to be more to my life than this. There would come a day when I would retire, and what would I do then? I didn't necessarily have the answers at this time, but I knew where I wanted to go.

I also realised that everything was now my responsibility. The buck stopped with me. People could help and advise me, but my decisions both good and bad were mine alone. If I found a way out of the space that I was in then it would have been my doing; likewise, if I continued to make poor and self-destructive decisions then that was also my doing. I wanted to be at the Tokyo 2020 Olympics more than anything. Gymnastics is in my blood. I needed my body to hold together but I knew I wanted to be there and it was now up to me.

Chapter 8

Ibiza Rescue

I felt I had made progress with my mental health during 2019 but not enough to truly move beyond it. It was such a hard year in so many ways, and as I approached October I still felt as though an enormous cloud was hanging over me. I felt burdened by pressure and expectation. My shoulder wasn't really progressing and the thought of not being able to make the Tokyo Olympics was haunting me. I was consumed by what this would mean for my life, my businesses and what people would think of me. With this weight on my shoulders and feeling permanently tired, I was still in a pretty dark place.

One of my best friends and teammates, Ash Watson, was also leaving the UK to join Cirque du Soleil in Canada, which I felt really sad about. Ash has been an incredible friend to me and actually a massive influence on me without him realising it. We were always training partners at Leeds Gymnastics Club, but also much more than that. His outlook and attitude towards his gymnastics was always so inspiring to me. We shared a room when we were with the national squad at Lilleshall and I often found him reading self-help books while in bed. He was so positive and fresh towards life, whatever was in front of him. He was also an incredible gymnast! Ash is the same age as Max Whitlock and won everything in the juniors. He just had horrific luck with injuries with four big surgeries on just one leg. We had had so many brilliant memories and laughs in and out of the gym and his leaving pushed my mood further down. In reality, it gave me an excuse to have a lot of nights out throughout that time to 'see him off'. It was fun, but I was just back in the same destructive cycle. I was battling with my mental health and the booze, once again, masked how I was truly feeling. I was 'OK', but I couldn't see how I could get beyond this.

Luke had mentioned to me previously that he wanted to take me away to Ibiza, where he and his fiancée have a house, for a week to help me work on some of my issues. Now my thoughts for Ibiza were party, party and more party, but Luke had a very different idea to what we would be doing! He has an amazing grasp of many of the issues I battle with and felt some time away, where it was just me and him, meant we could do a lot of work on them all. Luke is like a second father to me and I trust him with my life; I knew that a trip like this would be worthwhile. So just after Ash left for Canada, I called Luke and asked him if we could get this trip sorted. I needed something to get me out of the mental place I was in. I also needed to get out of Leeds to break the cycle I found myself in.

In the last week of October, Luke and I flew out to Ibiza. It is no exaggeration to say that this trip changed my life.

Luke's house is on the quiet side of the island and he had set out a daily routine for us that involved a training session in the gym, a meditation session, a self-awareness session and then another training session in the pool. However, the first thing he asked me to do was a 'water therapy' session that he had booked for me. He explained that it would be a one-on-one session with a water therapist in a Watsu pool, which is a heated hydrotherapy pool. To be honest, I had no idea what he was talking about but was just in a place that I was willing to try anything. Luke drove me over to the pool, which was in a rural part of the island, and I met Sophie, the water therapist, who explained that I would be in the water for about an hour with my eyes closed and she would move me around the water sometimes submerging me, but only ever in a way I was totally comfortable with. All I needed to do was close my eyes and let go. Luke also told me just to relax and let it all happen.

It is so difficult for me to explain what happened to me, but it was mind blowing.

Sophie moved my body through the water in a steady rhythm, sometimes on the surface and sometimes under the water. She held me in her arms and sometimes it felt like a dance. I just closed my eyes and relaxed. Time just drifted away, and I felt as if I was swimming deep in the ocean. Initially, I worried I wouldn't be able to keep my eyes closed for that length of time, but it wasn't even close to an issue. It was like the deepest meditation I had ever experienced. Every worry, every pressure, every burden and every expectation that I carried just drifted away. I felt like a child again. I felt this pure simplicity to life, it was just me without any ego or complication. The session was an hour long, but it felt as though I could have been there forever. I felt as if I was a child exploring the bottom of the ocean without a worry in the world. The feeling was actually … perfect … just pure bliss.

As Sophie pulled me to the surface for the end of the session, I felt deeply emotional. It was as though a weight had been lifted off me and I had viewed what life could be like without all the pressure I had on me. It felt as though I could reset everything in my head. As I looked at Sophie, I knew something extraordinary had happened to me (and you have to remember that this had been a session with a woman that I had never met before). Sophie explained that she could feel my energy in the water and she knew that it had a big impact on me.

Luke was waiting for me outside the pool. As I got in the car, I didn't know what to say. I was genuinely lost for words. But Luke had undergone one of these sessions himself and knew what I had experienced. He was so happy for me and we tried to make sense of it on the way back to the house. Luke explained that the feeling in the water is when life is pure and simple. We feel like children because it reminds us of being in the womb. Life is perfect without any sort of negativity. In meditation terms, it is called 'oneness', when it is just you without any sort of interfering emotion, ego or thought. It was a glimpse at what life can be centred on. Of course, life is complicated, with lots of challenges, but Luke explained that we can be centred on this sort of feeling whatever is going on around us and it will give us incredible strength to deal with challenges and pressures. Luke also explained, though, that this sort of therapy only gives us a view at what life can be like and we need to back it up with more work on ourselves. As we drove back to the house, I felt like a different person – relaxed, ready to rest and in a weird way, really optimistic about what could happen now.

It was the start of an incredible week for me. For months I hadn't been sleeping well. I wasn't going to sleep until the early hours and then struggled to get myself up for the start of training. It was one of the bad cycles I had got myself in, but that night I slept like a baby. In fact, I went on to sleep amazingly all week and this totally reset my sleeping patterns for when I went back home.

The next day, Luke and I started our little daily routine. He would wake me up about 10 a.m. with coffee and breakfast and then we would head to the gym. I would work out as Luke worked in the café. After the gym, we would grab some lunch and then head back to the house. The time together was amazing, we talked so much. We shared all our thoughts and it was like constant therapy with one of the people closest to me. Afternoons were meditation and self-awareness sessions, before another training session in the pool. I had meditated before at home in Leeds but always struggled with it a little. Luke helped me understand that it wasn't about 'trying' to meditate, it was actually about letting go and not interfering with the mind. Let thoughts come and go, like passing clouds in the sky, and actually don't 'try'. We meditated together, which probably sounds hilarious to all of you and not the normal athlete/agent dynamics! But it was amazing. It was all part of the lovely time I had with Luke, Jo, and their children. It was calm, peaceful and just so healthy.

The self-awareness sessions were huge for me. Luke focused on two main points for me with them. The first was how I defined myself in life. He pointed out that my entire self-worth and self-esteem had become centred on how I was doing with my gymnastics, which in turn led to how I was doing on social media. If those things were going well, then I felt good about myself, but if they weren't because, for example, I was injured, then I figuratively fell off a cliff with how I felt about myself. I couldn't cope with it. We did sessions where Luke asked me what sort of person I would like to be remembered as and as I wrote down how I felt, we built a picture of how I would like to be. He challenged me to understand that we can be as motivated as ever to be successful, but we don't need to define ourselves by it. Luke explained that when he changed this in his mindset, he actually became more successful with business. He didn't get carried away with successes and didn't fall apart during tough times. He led with his heart in a logical manner, making good decisions, and, importantly, led a much happier life. I realised that I could put every part of my being into winning an Olympic gold medal and whether or not I did, I could still live a happy and healthy life because I wanted my life to be defined by the type of person I was: the son, the brother, the friend, the role model, the person to others around me. I suddenly realised that Nile was a person, a human being, a spirit who happened to be a gymnast, an influencer and a businessman. I had got muddled into believing I was everything the other way around. My successes in the gym, on social media or in business meant I was a good person. I had got obsessed by views and likes on social media and fed off the success that drove. My gymnastics led all of that, so being badly injured affected everything and I couldn't cope as it hit me right in my core of self-worth. Luke helped me turn that around in my mind. It might all sound so simple but when you are caught in that cycle, it is so hard to see. The space and time in Ibiza allowed me to realise this, It wasn't a light-bulb moment; it was much bigger than that. It felt like a life-changing moment.

The second thing Luke worked with me on was understanding what we meant by 'ego'. So often I have thought that sportsmen and women needed big egos to perform on the big stage. Cristiano Ronaldo or Conor McGregor being the epitome of that vision. There is an element of truth in that, but Luke explained that actually that was often confusing ego with true confidence. They are not necessarily the same thing. The ego was actually a much bigger and more damaging thing than I realised. For example, defining myself by how many views I got on YouTube was me leading with my ego, and it meant I was chasing something that would never truly satisfy me. If my girlfriend and I argued, and I said something that I didn't really mean because I just wanted to win the argument, then I was leading with my ego; again, it would never lead to something positive in my life. If I was injured and fell apart mentally, it was because I was leading with my ego because I couldn't cope with what people thought of me. In that case, ego actually came from fear. So we worked on me being able to identify when I led with my ego and how I could instead lead with my heart. How I could replace those destructive times, when my ego was out of control, with times when I led with my heart and tried to just be the best version of me. The phrasing 'leading with your heart' sounds a bit soft and a bit like a teenager with a crush, but Luke explained that it really wasn't. Leading with your heart can be calm, clear and logical, but you just always want to present the best version of yourself to the world. It all made perfect sense to me and I could see a way forward with it.

All this meant two things for me. Firstly, from now on, I had to own all my decisions and behaviour. I understood now how my mind worked and could be a witness to my thought patterns. I couldn't make excuses, I had to own whatever I did. If I had a big night out then I couldn't use an excuse for it, such as I was struggling with being injured, I had to recognise what I was doing and what it would lead to. Secondly, and very importantly, I now realised that all the darkness I felt was because I was walking around with an enormous burden and pressure on my shoulders. I couldn't cope with being injured and it was taking me to a place, not helped by booze and gambling, that meant I couldn't see a way out. The time in Ibiza with Luke gave me an entirely different perspective and an opportunity to let go of all of that. It was massive for me.

I returned to England in November and the next two months were so positive. My relationships with my family and friends improved, plus I got back together with my girlfriend. I worked so hard on everything Luke and I discussed. I trained regularly and pushed my shoulder sensibly but that little bit more. Importantly, the shoulder started to make progress. Now, I don't know if that physical progress was linked to my mental progress, but part of me thinks it was. Did my mind let go and start to be positive, so my body followed? Quite possibly. I started to see light in everything I was doing. I knew that 2020 was going to be an enormous challenge for me. To get my shoulder and body right to qualify for the Olympics was going to be tough. Many people had already written me off. But I could see how I was going to do it. With each push of the shoulder, I was improving. My new mindset meant I felt bulletproof and the drinking and gambling faded away.

Another crucial thing happened on 9 December 2019 – Russia was banned as a team from the Tokyo Olympics due to doping violations. This had a big impact on my chances of making Tokyo. With Russia not there, Team GB had a significant chance of winning an Olympic medal while in the mix with China, Japan and the USA. And Olympic medals are priceless to Olympic sports. If we now had a significantly larger chance of winning a medal in the team event, then this would have a big impact on team selection for the four places available. The team would need to focus on All-Arounders like me, who could contribute to the team, rather than just specialists. This was really significant, and everything felt as if it was turning for me.

After a New Year's Eve holiday in Dubai, I came back to England in 2020; a very different man to the one that entered 2019. Mentally, I was thriving on the fact that most people had written me off. I knew I could get there and so did the people closest to me. And I knew that once I got to the Olympics, I would be a very dangerous competitor for others – especially if they hadn't anticipated that I would be there. I began getting this vision of me walking on to the plane to Tokyo and putting my bag in the hold above the seats and then looking around and smiling at the other gymnasts and coaches with a look that said 'I know you didn't think I would be here but I knew I always would be.' I had never felt so strong mentally and physically, I was improving with every day.

It felt as though everything that could go wrong in 2019 had gone wrong, but as I sat there looking forward to an Olympic year, I was glad it all happened. I had started to fall apart as a result, but it had given me the opportunity to rebuild myself into a better version. A version of myself that was happy and healthy and ready to take on challenges without being consumed by the meaning of the outcomes. I was just so grateful for the people around me, who showed me patience and love when I wasn't behaving as I should have been. They all helped me find a way out of it.

I was ready for 2020.

Chapter 9

Addictive Behaviours

Writing this book has actually been a massive eye-opener for me; I see that my addictive behaviour patterns have been apparent through my entire life. In some ways, it is no wonder I ended up with some of the difficulties I have.

My dad reminds me that when I was a kid, he often read a bedtime story to me. Nothing unusual in this but I used to make him read exactly the same story every single night for months on end. It was as though I was fixated on that one particular story. My love for it moved into an obsession and I just couldn't get enough of it. As a child, I must have had a sense that this story would make me happy and I would fall asleep.

My obsessive and addictive tendencies have been there all along, although this wasn't all bad. I immediately got hooked on gymnastics and was addicted to learning and perfecting new skills. I loved to perform and compete; it was another obsession. This all definitely helped me become the gymnast I am today. Even if I look back to the first time I watched YouTube, it immediately became an obsession! I just couldn't get enough of watching gymnastics videos online, which wasn't necessarily a bad thing either.

The thing I can see now is how these behaviours eventually manifested themselves in a negative way. I guess some of my strengths have actually become my weakness. For example, the 16-year-old who went to Montpellier for the European Junior Championships, completely obsessed with getting the results that everyone, including myself, was pushing for, had also developed a serious eating disorder. I can look back now and understand that it was a way of me believing I was injecting some control into what I was doing. I was obsessed with achieving what I needed to, and that pressure needed some sort of outlet. Control of my weight was a way of controlling the pressure. I would eat less and less, resulting in me losing weight; I told myself that the lighter I was, the better I would be at gymnastics. It was like a simple formula.

But then, like any addictive behaviour, you realise that the feeling of control is actually an illusion. The behaviour is then controlling you and the pressure builds again. There's no balance in place. No outlet to manage everything. And in this case, the blowout from that pressure came in the form of binge eating. A vicious cycle that was all about trying to control things and actually leading to me lacking control. Just horrible.

Once my eating disorder was in some ways sorted, gambling came into my life. It was just another outlet for the pressure that built up in me through my obsession to achieve great things in the gym. Initially, it gave me that brilliant feeling and released the pressure, but then, just like my eating disorder, it became an obsession and started controlling me. I couldn't get away from it and the escalation was rapid.

Once gambling was addressed in the build-up to the Rio Olympics, guess what? There was something new – drinking. And the same pattern happened all over again.

In the run up to Rio, I started to go out every Saturday night in Leeds. I know I'm not meant to admit that, but it's true. I had a day off from training on Sunday, so Saturday night was my release. Every Saturday was a big night. Again, release from the pressure of everything I was doing. And just like with every other addictive behaviour I ever have shown, to start with, it was brilliant. I had fun and everything was under some sort of control. I actually had some quite strict rules with my drinking at that time – only vodka and soda so as not to put weight on, and there was a protein bar and hydration tablet waiting for me by my bed when I got home! And just as with every other addictive behaviour I have ever shown, eventually it took its grip on me. After the Rio Olympics, the celebrations went on for weeks and then months. A major blowout was never far away at all. I just couldn't get away from it. Eventually, through hard training, I would wrestle myself out of the cycle, but it was never far away. When I got hit with my injuries, the drinking came back. Drinking was my release, my friend to start with, but then it began to control me, and I 'needed' it to cope. It was terrifying, to be honest.

The same pattern. Again and again. All my life. It was always there. It was just the type of behaviour that changed over time.

However, I was still achieving some great things in the gym; that was in some ways what gave me and the people around me a false impression of how bad my cycles of behaviour were. It couldn't be that bad if I went and won Great Britain's first Olympic medal in the High Bar, could it?!

I have worked so much with my manager, Luke, on this, and we both feel passionately about how there needs to be a better understanding of this in elite sport. Far too often we look into elite sport and think that if someone is performing well that nothing could be going 'that' wrong in their life. It's just not true. The patterns of behaviour that were helping me rise up and progress through the gymnastics world were also slowly, sometimes quickly, destroying me.

The truth is that elite sport is basically focused on outcomes. In gymnastics, that means medals and they mean millions of pounds to the sport. If we are winning, then all is good. If we are losing, then things need to be looked at, and to be honest, this is what happened to me. The biggest investigations into my behaviour were when something went wrong – I got another injury, or I wasn't responding well to recovering from an injury – but my patterns had been there for all to see for a long time. Please don't misunderstand me, this isn't anyone's fault, I own my decisions, but this is just the culture of elite sport at the moment. Everyone is driving toward outcomes and if those outcomes are being achieved, then nothing can be too badly wrong. But from my own experiences, the picture is much bigger than that. If I hadn't had some good people around me to help me see my patterns of behaviour, then what would have happened? I may have won Olympic gold, but my life would have fallen apart in retirement. Surely that can't be quite right?

At the start of 2020, I was desperate to make the Tokyo Olympics and win gold. I knew I had a massive challenge to overcome with my shoulder, but I was totally focused on what I wanted to achieve. I knew what 'outcome' I wanted, but the key point around this is what would happen if this didn't happen? For example, what if it was out of my control because I picked up another injury? Would I just self-combust because that outcome I wanted wasn't possible? Was my entire perception of happiness and self-worth hanging on to this outcome? This is the sort of mentality we demand of our athletes – we want a team of winners, right? Yes of course we do, but at what cost? The cost is our mental well-being and everything that comes with that when it deteriorates. And is that mentality of 'all or nothing' on an outcome truly necessary? It really isn't, in my opinion. I can be completely dedicated to what I want to achieve, but be able to have a broader outlook on life as well. It means I can be a winner AND healthy. At times, we get glimpses of this in sport when someone talks about real pressure: being a soldier fighting in a war or someone struggling to feed their family, rather than being on a sporting field, but often the reaction from media and fans can be a question mark around 'how much they want it'. The reality is that in Olympic sports, where funding is intrinsically linked to medals, the primary focus, by a long way, is outcomes.

In my case, my mentality around outcomes and the pressure they brought was so important to my well-being. If this was off and started to lose all balance, then my addictive behaviours could return really quickly. I would feel the pressure of the outcomes and then be swamped in anxiety that would need a release, in my case either alcohol or gambling, and then a vicious cycle would have started. My poor mental health led to my behaviours and then my poor behaviours led to my worsening mental health.

This always seems to have a negative slant on it, i.e., it is if something bad happens. And this is obviously a massive trigger but, in my case, it is also when good things happen. Luke and I talked through what would happen if I won Olympic gold and how we would ensure I didn't just fall off a cliff. There is also a pressure release when you win and that can actually be equally dangerous for me. Of course, I would want to celebrate an amazing result, but Luke and I also planned for me to go to Ibiza again with him and have a week away from everything if all went perfectly. Suddenly in my life I realised the importance of me staying mentally well. Without it, I really had nothing. I had learnt about myself that using my strengths in life was a fine line to tread. I was capable of a lot in and out of the gym and that obsessiveness drove me forward in life; left unwatched, it could also eventually take me to dark places.

I actually feel incredibly lucky to have discovered this about myself in my early twenties. I have so much of my life ahead of me and I now have a real feel for who I want to be and how I want to live my life. I know I can achieve great things, but it doesn't have to be at the expense of my health.

As time has gone on, I have also realised that all of this will be a work in progress. There is no quick fix. My addictive and obsessive nature will always be with me and sometimes it will be more of a problem than at other times. The lockdown months of Covid have been a massive challenge for me because so many days have just felt the same. Like everyone else across the globe, so many days have felt like Groundhog Day and well … just beige. I have really had to watch myself in these moments because when I am mentally not in a great place, I can reach out for the wrong thing to pick me up and then suddenly I can be in a bad pattern again. I really have to watch my behaviours and thought processes.

I am lucky to have amazing family and friends around me and a manager like Luke who understands all this better than anyone. Going forward, I really want to play a role in helping people who find themselves with similar sorts of destructive patterns in their life. I will always try to be an honest voice on social media about it all, but I would also love to have a role in something more specific that helps sportspeople, because I don't believe these issues will be leaving elite sport any time soon.

Chapter 10

Leeds Gymnastics Club

I felt I had come a long way mentally at the end of 2019, but it is fair to say that 2020 couldn't have got off to a worse start.

I had been at Leeds Gymnastics Club since I was 5 years old and trained with my coach, Dave Murray, through every junior and senior international event I had ever competed in. The club was a big part of my life and supported me a great deal. They had, of course, also celebrated me as I was the club's only ever Olympic medallist, and I have always felt that I have given a lot back to the club in exposure and credibility.

Yet, what happened at the end of 2019 and start of 2020 meant I could never go back there.

Before I explain what happened, it pains me that I can't explicitly say who this person is at Leeds Gymnastics Club for legal reasons. It infuriates me that this person is able to carry on with their position of authority at the club while protected by a board and a system that refuses to understand how low they stoop just to protect their own self-interests. If they took a moment to look out from their closed bubble, they would see what a disgrace the club has become. Everyone surrounding Leeds Gymnastics Club knows who this individual is and despite numerous complaints, mine being one, this person still continues to hold power over coaches and gymnasts at the club. As I can't say who this person is, I will refer to them as 'Individual X' or 'X' for short. I will also refer to Individual X as 'they or them' so as to be non-gender specific.

I attended the Leeds Gymnastics Club Christmas drinks party in Leeds on 19 December 2019. Most of the club staff were my friends and it was a party I had always attended since I was allowed to. The only member of staff who I seemed to have a constant problem with was Individual X, who is still one of the club's administrators. Actually, to be more accurate, they always seemed to have a problem with me. Why that was the case, I'm not 100 per cent certain, but what I am sure of, though, is that Individual X had been gunning for me for a while.

Individual X is a really difficult person to warm to. X barely cracked a smile for me or for anyone else for that matter and is what you might describe as an 'energy sapper'. You rarely, if ever, felt better having spoken to them. Almost all the coaches had an issue with X but often weren't brave enough to speak up for fear of losing their jobs. I had a few run-ins with X over the years, mainly due to the amount of filming and vlogging I wanted to do in the gym. Various procedures needed to be handled correctly and I hold my hands up to say that often in my rush, I didn't always get this right, which resulted in X's wrath. In the end, we had a system that meant I had to ask permission via Luke whenever I wanted some filming in the gym. We seemed to get there with it all, but I always felt as if I had a target on my back when it came to X.

Matters didn't seem to be helped when we opened our first Nile Wilson Gymnastics Club in Rotherham in September 2019. Despite the gym being some 35 miles away from Leeds, there was definitely a cold feeling towards me about it. This was especially the case when Tom Rawlinson, who was one of my coaches and one of Leeds Gymnastics Club's best, left the club to join our gym in Rotherham. We were well within our rights to recruit whom we wanted, but Tom was the only coach who left Leeds to join us. Looking back, X clearly spent more time stewing over the fact that they thought we had 'poached' Tom, rather than analysing why he left.

The Leeds Gymnastics Club Christmas drinks party was at a bar in Leeds and X was there as well as me. I was standing at the bar, in conversation with a couple of the coaches, when X rushed towards me and grabbed my wrist and pulled me hard away from the bar. I was in shock and resisted to begin with, so they just persisted in pulling my wrist. Incidentally, this was the wrist I had surgery on a couple of months previously. Eventually, with X tugging on my wrist, I moved away from the bar and the group I was in, and X was in my face, shouting, 'How dare you try and poach my fucking coaches! You need to fucking leave now!'

I genuinely thought X was joking and laughed as I said, 'Yeah, very funny X.'

But there was no humour in X's face when replying, 'I'm not being funny; I will throw you out.'

X kept saying these things, all the time pointing in my face. Pure aggression was etched across their face and in their voice. I didn't quite know what to do.

To give you some context around this: our gym in Rotherham was badly flooded in freak localised weather that November and was closed until April 2020. Whether we wanted to recruit coaches or not, we had nowhere for them to go to work! We were battling away to keep the current staff on our payroll as we had no income due to the closure. Even if it had been put to me in a non-aggressive manner, X's accusation was completely ridiculous.

In disbelief, I started to walk away from them to go back to my friends at the bar and as I turned, X reached for me again. I just wanted to get away from this horrible person. Unfortunately, X wasn't going to let up this easily and followed me back to the bar, putting an arm around my shoulders to get themself in front of me again. They then pushed me in the chest and marched me backwards 4 or 5 metres away from the bar. It was just nastiness in my face and I wanted to get away. I tried walking back to the bar again, but, like the first time, they followed me to confront me while pressed against the bar and repeatedly told me that I needed to leave the bar.

I was completely shell-shocked. One of the club's administrators was physically trying to get me to leave the bar, at the same time making ludicrous accusations. The truth was that most of the Leeds' coaches were asking me about our gym in Rotherham because they were all interested in it – as you would be as a gymnastics coach! Regardless of that, I was deeply upset by what X had done to me and I left the bar shortly afterwards, in total shock.

After all the work Luke and I had done on my mental well-being, I tried not to react quickly and thought about it for a night before telling Luke and my dad what had happened. Both of them were totally shocked to hear what I described. At this point, I realised that the bar probably had CCTV footage of the incident, so I went back to the bar and asked them to look – and sure enough, they had the footage.

It was incredible to watch. After everything that gymnastics as a sport has been through, here was an administrator using physical force against a gymnast in a public place without the slightest thought that this might be grossly inappropriate or just down right wrong! In the months leading up to this incident, I had had surgery on my wrist and my neck – areas of my body that were both affected by this confrontation. The manner of the incident made it very clear that Individual X hadn't given this a moment's thought.

I sent the footage to Luke and my dad, and they couldn't believe it. It was appalling. It was awful to experience and watch, and after all my mental health battles of 2019, I was still in shock that someone in X's position would do this to me. There were hundreds of different ways the situation could have been handled; in no way was this acceptable.

We all agreed that I needed to lodge an official grievance with the club, but weren't entirely sure how to do that. However, I called Andy Firth, a board member at the club, three days after the incident, to request a time to see him. Andy informed me that he didn't have time to see me before Christmas. Whether Andy was aware of the incident via X is a question worth investigating, but he definitely wasn't rushing to help me. I felt hurt and angry by this point. X's actions couldn't have gone unnoticed by others at the club, bearing in mind the bar was packed with the club's staff. X may have mentioned it to Andy as well, anticipating that something might come of it. But for that moment, the club definitely wasn't rushing to address it.

I talked through every possible option with Luke and my dad; writing a formal letter to lodge my grievance to the board of the club seemed the next logical step. I had no confidence in Andy being involved due to his lack of urgency to help me after my call, and made it clear in my letter that I didn't want him involved with this.

My complaint, in any context, was a really serious one. Gymnastics has suffered from a history of gymnasts not being treated well and here I was alleging that a person in authority at the club had used inappropriate physical force on me; and that I had video evidence. You would think that the club would rush to get on top of this. You would think wrong.

The club acknowledged receipt of my first email on 2 January 2020. Five days later, on 7 January, I had heard nothing and had to chase. I was told I would be contacted in the next couple of days, once the club received legal advice. Bearing in mind that I hadn't even presented my case, this 'legal advice' was a puzzle. Anyway, guess what? By 15 January I had still heard nothing and had to chase again. It was nothing short of a disgrace in my mind and whether correct or not, it felt as if there was scrambling behind the scenes to try to find a way for this to disappear as quickly as possible. That is just how I felt, although I believe I can be forgiven for thinking that – bearing in mind a serious incident had happened to me, followed by me being fobbed off on the phone by Andy Firth and then not receiving a proper response to my first email for two weeks.

Finally, on 16 January I was informed that I could attend an investigation meeting on 20 January with two board members so they could hear my side of the story, but I was also informed that

> If it makes you more comfortable the meeting can take place away from the gym. You may bring one person with you.

However, that person needs to be aware that they are attending the meeting in a support role and can play no active part in the meeting. They may take notes for example, but will not be able to answer or ask any questions. I trust this is OK.

I was nervous about this entire process and had already raised my doubts to the club about the impartiality of the investigation. I had to chase for three weeks for any action to take place and was now being told that someone could come with me but they were not allowed to ask any questions. It felt as though the blows kept coming. Nothing about how this was being handled filled us with any confidence that it would be done so appropriately.

I attended the meeting with my dad, and it seemed to be handled reasonably well by the two board members. However, there was one moment that made me realise that all my fears about this were going to come true. I was asked what I would like to happen, and I responded that I thought X should be dismissed. Both board members looked physically shocked by me saying that. Yet, if you were looking at this incident impartially, you would have to take this into consideration. Why would you look so visibly shocked by the suggestion unless you had no intention of seeing that happen? I showed them the CCTV footage, but as far as the investigation went that was the end of my part in it. In fact, the 'investigation' was wrapped up in fewer than ten days and the 'findings' were emailed to me on 2 February.

They concluded:

- As you yourself stated, the initial contact with you, by the wrist, was an attempt by X to gain your attention to discuss an issue of concern (i.e. the content of your discussion with a current LGC staff member at the bar).
- There is no evidence at all to suggest that X struck you at any time.

- After responding to X, who was trying to make a point to you, you walked away back to the bar. X's attempt to regain your attention as you were facing away from them led to your further claim of physical assault causing harm to your neck. It is clear that witnesses perceived this action to be an attempt by X to gain your attention as they were very angry/upset about something.
- An attempt by X to push you toward the door to throw you out of the party was not witnessed by staff and friends present who only became aware of your upset upon hearing your account of proceedings.
- Despite your view that X acted in an extreme way on that evening, there is no evidence that any 'bullying' has taken place.
- Similarly, in relation to the claim that X's behaviour had been discriminatory, there is no evidence to support this with the investigation team being of the opinion that similar conclusions would have been drawn irrespective of the gender of those involved.
- As CCTV footage shows that surrounding staff involved in their own conversations were unaware of the happenings in very close proximity to them, we can only conclude that the alleged incident was a much more low-key argument than was suggested in your letter.

They finished by confirming that no disciplinary action would be taken against Individual X.

Let me repeat that – there would be no disciplinary action taken. Zero. None. Not even an acknowledgement that their actions were inappropriate.

In fact, it was virtually positioned that X's actions were justified considering how upset they were.

It was truly astonishing. I would challenge anyone to watch the CCTV footage and not walk away utterly shocked that they were watching a gymnastics club administrator doing that to a gymnast of the club. Actually, I would challenge anyone to watch the CCTV footage, go through the list of conclusions from the 'investigation', and not feel shocked.

The vast majority of the club's basis for their conclusions was based on what witnesses said they saw and felt, despite the whole thing being on camera! These are witnesses who would be nervous about the possible consequences of speaking out against X. It was also a packed bar so people's view of the incident would not be as accurate as actually watching it on the CCTV footage.

The most telling part of it all was that the club couldn't even acknowledge that X's actions were inappropriate. It said it all.

I was absolutely devastated.

I couldn't believe that the club I had proudly represented this whole time would just hang me out to dry in an incident that they should be all over. It was horrendous.

Throughout the whole of January, when I walked into the gym, I prayed I wouldn't see X. Unfortunately, I did a few times and there was never even a hint of apology from them. As far as they and the club were concerned, what happened in the bar that night was my fault. Entirely my fault. Just like so many gymnasts in the past – I was the problem. Not the administrator.

I had worked so hard to get my mental well-being back to a good place but now I had to decide what to do to protect it from a process point of view and for my gymnastics. I had no confidence in the process. I didn't think it was impartial and an appeal process would just be kicking the can down the road until they told me the same thing, while all the time I had this hanging over me. British Gymnastics palmed this off as a 'club matter' and I will come back to this in the next chapter. I just couldn't take the risk of being affected by a poor excuse of an investigation while I needed to train my arse off during some crucial weeks.

From a gymnastics point of view, I felt I had no option but to consider leaving Leeds. The environment at the club felt toxic. I was surrounded by people who didn't really care about me and with X never far away from me. How could I continue training there? An environment where I should feel comfortable to push myself now felt horrible. Really horrible. I felt let down and completely isolated.

My email response to the findings of the 'investigation' did not hold back,

> I am bitterly disappointed by the findings and the manner in which this investigation has been handled. It has confirmed every fear I had about the administration at Leeds Gymnastics Club. The outcome of the grievance does not reflect the discussion we had during the investigation. Despite submitting overwhelming evidence with CCTV footage, that has not been referenced in the summary other than your belief it has little relevance. I have a complete lack of confidence in the Leeds Gymnastics board to have the capability and knowledge to handle a grievance of this nature in the appropriate manner. I will not validate this process any more because it is flawed, biased and some of the findings are at best nonsensical and at worst shameful. I can assure the board that this will not be the end of the matter as far as I am concerned. I will continue to pursue that this case is given the impartial attention it deserves for the sake of Leeds Gymnastics Club community and gymnastics in general. Gymnastics has so many challenges in overcoming the historical nature of how gymnasts have been treated by coaches and administrators, unfortunately this is a shocking example of how little it has changed. I am upset but also embarrassed for the club.

> I won't be putting myself through the appeal process and I won't be attending the meeting to discuss the 'investigation' that apparently took place. This outcome shows that the investigation was not impartial but illogical so cannot be trusted moving forward. I believe there has been a complete lack of support and empathy towards me following the shocking incident that took place. This incident and subsequent handling of the grievance has directly impacted my well-being and mental health.

There was no way I could continue training at Leeds any more.

A conference call was arranged between myself, my dad, Luke, Baz Collie and Dave Murray. The reality was that if I moved clubs, I would have to step away from Dave as my coach, which really wasn't great. Dave was employed full-time by Leeds. The conversation centred around me making sure I made a decision based on what was right for my gymnastics and me and not based on sticking two fingers up at Leeds. But how I felt about the environment at the club, including feeling angry and hurt, played a significant role in my decision. There was no way I was going to be able to train properly in that sort of toxicity.

There was the option for me to move to Manchester to a gym where Giarni Regini-Moran had been training. It was an excellent gym and they were happy to have me. It meant me having to stay in Manchester during the week, but the whole thing just felt fresh and I was excited about it. I felt a buzz about starting there. I would also travel to Lilleshall from time to time, and Baz was going to come to Manchester for sessions. It would take some adjusting but it was doable. The only thing missing was how I would have time with Dave and that wasn't ideal, but we agreed we would find a way.

I had to give everything I could towards the next three months to give myself the best chance at competing at both the English and British Championships in April. If I could compete in the All-Around at both of those then I stood a chance at selection for the European Championships, and from there to the Olympics.

Leeds left me no choice and challenged the mental stability I had worked so hard at maintaining. Life has a habit of challenging us from all angles, but I never imagined that I would be made to feel this way by my home gymnastics club.

I had to cut ties, but it didn't mean I would leave this incident to the laughable judgement of the club's 'investigation'. When the time was right for me and my training, I would make my voice heard on this.

Chapter 11

British Gymnastics

Heading towards the originally scheduled 2020 Olympic Games in Tokyo, I was one of British Gymnastics' best medal-winning hopes. Olympic medals for UK Sport funded sports are worth a huge amount of money. So when I felt I had to leave my home gymnastics club after a serious complaint, and therefore be away from my coach, you would think that British Gymnastics (BG) would be anxious to get the whole thing resolved? Well, there was absolutely no urgency about it from anyone at the top of BG.

My two coaches, Baz Collie and Dave Murray, were involved in the discussions, but no one else at BG contacted me. With only months to go to an Olympic Games, this was a really big deal for one of BG's most important gymnasts, and yet, no call from the performance director. I have been subsequently told that at the BG board meeting led by the CEO, Jane Allen, in which this matter was discussed, the attitude was 'well, this might be good to knock him down a peg or two'. I was devastated by the way Leeds Gymnastics Club had treated me, but this secondary shrug of the shoulders by BG was just another knife in my back. I had given so much to the sport – my body and mind had both suffered greatly. I had helped propel the sport forward and yet, there was a vacuum of support from BG. Was it because they thought I wasn't as important any more due to my injuries? Or did they just not really care? Was I just another piece of meat to help them win medals and they would move on to the next when I was finished with? It was utterly heartbreaking.

I had written to Leeds Gymnastics Club on 5 February 2020 to say that I wouldn't validate an appeal or mediation process and had absolutely no confidence in a process that we had to force to get started after four weeks – and then had made a sweeping decision in less than ten days. I had copied Aaron Prior, the Conduct and Disciplinary Manager at BG, into that email.

On 6 February, Aaron replied to me and included a threat over going public and saying that this should remain a Leeds Gymnastic Club matter. He said:

> I would like to make clear to all, that while this is clearly a very emotive situation for all parties, I do not expect that this issue is played out in the public or online arena more than is fair and necessary and should this be the case, we will consider any further action that may be necessary against any party.

> From our perspective, should either side wish to, we can review the process including any evidence that was considered and will provide comment on the process and the outcome. To be clear; we are not in a position to overturn the outcome but to make recommendations, where we believe it appropriate for the panel, you as the complainant and the club as the respondent to consider.

I was totally isolated. BG were clearly not going to get involved significantly and had already threatened me about going public before even getting close to understanding my complaint. Whose side was Aaron on?

On 11 February, I wrote to Aaron Prior:

> Good morning Aaron,

> I would like you and your team to undertake a review of this grievance and process, how would that work and when?

My priority now is getting into a routine and working as hard as I can towards competitions that are coming up in order to focus 100 per cent on making the Olympic team. I would rather this was put on hold for a period of time while I focus on that. Is that possible?

I have made it clear why I have declined the appeal process with Leeds.

Nile

On 28 February, we still hadn't heard from Aaron, so I chased him again and emailed James Thomas, the performance director at BG, asking for his help. I got no reply. I just wanted things to be settled so I could get on with my training and move forward.

Despite no reply to my email of 11 February, in which I asked for time to concentrate on my training, we suddenly received a letter from Aaron Prior on 3 March. It said:

I have concluded that the investigation was undertaken appropriately and there is no evidence to suggest that the outcome is not appropriate and I will not be making any further recommendations to the club other than those I have already included in this letter.

The conclusion was effectively that Individual X's accusation that I was trying to poach coaches was justified and X's actions not inappropriate in the circumstances.

As I write this, it still shocks me. There was no help. Nothing. And during this entire thing, no one at BG asked to come and see me, my dad or my manager. No one. We were just dismissed and effectively told to get on with it. Apparently, X's behaviour towards

me (or to any gymnast for that matter) was acceptable. I had asked
Aaron to hold off as I needed to concentrate on my training, and I was
ignored. The fact that I was a medal hope would make this really odd,
but I was not asking for special treatment, just basic support that
I would hope any gymnast would be afforded.

The truth is that gymnasts were always ignored. We were always
the problem.

Aaron Prior also stated:

> Having reviewed these, as well as the CCTV footage you have
> provided, I am not of the view that X was overtly aggressive
> in their physical approach to you. In fact, when they tried to
> take your attention from the group you were with, you clearly
> hold on to the bar to prevent this, causing them to have to use
> more force to pull you away.

Was I really being told that it was my fault that X had to use the
physical force they did on me because I resisted? And all of this was
being conducted via email when I had asked that there was a pause on
everything. It was heartbreaking to read from people that were meant
to be there to support me. I genuinely did my best to find peace with
this over the next few months, but I just couldn't. It felt so typical of
BG. Individual X was still doing their job, and still is today, with zero
repercussions. They had nothing to answer for, yet I was told that
I was the problem.

I wanted to get on with my training and move forward but this
whole thing kept coming back at me in my head. It was flat out wrong,
and I was sitting there taking it. During some of my most difficult
moments with my mental health, it haunted me. I found it so hard
to let go of. Once in a while I mentioned to Luke that I wanted to do
something in the media about it, but he was cautious about doing so.
It was a big deal to take on the gymnastics' authorities and he was

sensitive to exposing me to that. I understood but I could never find any peace with the whole thing.

But then came a change – Athlete A.

Towards the end of June, Netflix released the documentary *Athlete A*, which showed the appalling scale of abuse that American gymnasts had been forced to endure in recent years and the way that US Gymnastics had done little or nothing to stop it. Everything started to shift from there. Suddenly gymnasts across the world felt a freedom to speak up, including some very brave female British ones. It was as if the tide had shifted and gymnasts were finally now in a position of strength to say something. I watched as the media coverage intensified throughout July as more gymnasts were heard. I also watched the reaction of BG, which only reinforced the sad truth of the situation. Amy Tinkler had been shockingly ignored as the governing body just appeared to go into its usual damage limitation exercise. The CEO Jane Allen was, typically, nowhere to be seen.

I now knew that it was my time to say something.

I knew the risks. I would face a backlash from those within the institutions of Leeds Gymnastics Club and British Gymnastics looking to protect their precious reputations. But I also knew the impact my words would have. I was the first male gymnast to say anything and I was a genuine medal hope. I also had a huge online audience that I would share this with. I knew that I could move the dial of this topic very significantly.

Luke and I discussed it a lot and he immediately wanted me to do the interview with Dan Roan from the BBC. A majority of the media attention on the complaints from gymnasts had been driven by ITV, but Luke was adamant that we should go to Dan and the BBC. His reasoning was that Dan had a sizeable reputation for bringing to light big stories like this. He had previously done it with British Cycling. He didn't shirk big questions or difficult moments so my interview with him wouldn't be seen as an easy ride. It would also set the bar for the standard of interview that Jane Allen would need to match if she was going to be taken seriously within this discussion. This would play a huge factor in the weeks to come. Also, Luke wanted the BBC because he felt that would give the interview the biggest exposure possible, so we went ahead and lined up everything with Dan.

On 10 August my interview with Dan was released: 'British gymnasts are treated like pieces of meat'. That was my quote from the interview that went all across the world. The media coverage was mind blowing, and the interview had the impact I hoped it would.

The interview was a hugely emotional experience for me because I didn't realise how much I had been pre-conditioned to not say anything as a gymnast and here I was speaking up against the authorities who I had competed for from a very young age. It was also a release from all the hurt and isolation I had felt since the incident with Individual X from Leeds and BG.

And yet both organisations still tried to minimise it, or in Leeds' case even lie their way around it, rather than truly front up to it all. BG briefed people off the record that my incident really wasn't that big a deal and when the BBC approached Leeds for a quote to go with my interview, part of their original statement read that the conclusion of my case had been 'independently verified'. That was just a blatant lie.

The only other party to have reviewed my case was BG – hardly 'independent' in the circumstances – and it is worth noting that Aaron Prior actually wrote this in his final email to me:

> If I could offer any criticism in regard to process, I would have suggested a third, entirely independent panellist, although I recognise that this is not a simple thing to arrange. Regardless of this, I am satisfied that the process the club have followed was robust and proper.

I would like you to ask yourself these questions about Leeds – if everything was so above board and there was nothing to hide, then why was there a need to lie about this? Why were they scrambling to gain credibility in their position on it all if they were blameless?

The BBC didn't actually release that part of Leeds' statement, but it was in there. Leeds' board members also embarked on demeaning my character and briefing journalists that I had actually been kicked out of the club rather than leaving on my own free will. I expected this sort of thing to some extent but it still shocked me.

The reason I spoke up wasn't just about my incident at Leeds, it was because of the overall culture that existed in British Gymnastics. My incident bore no comparison to the physical and sexual abuse that others have suffered but, for me, it highlighted exactly what was wrong within our culture. A culture of fear and lack of genuine care for gymnasts was, in my opinion, driven primarily from the CEO, Jane Allen. It filtered down the organisation alarmingly. Sadly, my example was just one of hundreds where gymnasts were left feeling isolated and uncared for. The gymnast always came second or third after protecting the reputation of the institution. If we spoke up about anything, from relatively small things like the beds we had to sleep in, to medium things like performance bonuses, or to big things like suffering from verbal or physical abuse at training, we were always made to feel the same way: we were the problem and we should just be lucky to be doing what we were doing. The fear of non-selection was constantly held over us. We were conditioned in this and without realising it, we all fell into line with it. Maybe I did for a period of time after my experience with my complaint.

Gymnastics is the greatest sport in the world but there are some crucial things for us to remember when looking at this whole area. Gymnasts are younger in age than most other sportspeople when they reach an elite level. A gymnast could be well on the way in an elite programme at just 7, 8 or 9 years old. And, at times, gymnastics is extremely painful to the body, so you have to be pushed. Would a child of 7 or 8 go through that pain without being pushed? I don't think so. As part of this, gymnasts develop a huge reliance on their coaches. They get 'told' what to do all the time. To master a skill takes a huge amount of repetition and young gymnasts will be instructed to do that, rather than go off and do it themselves. So if you take this all into account, you'll understand that the lines between a healthy training environment and one that steps into anything inappropriate are very fine. I have already talked about how as a young gymnast I was scared of some of my coaches, but that's not because those coaches were bad people, it was just the way the coaching environment was back then and how people believed you produced elite gymnasts. It is not easy being a gymnastics coach. Gymnastics is an incredibly difficult sport and requires huge commitment. If coaches don't lead the drive towards achieving excellence, then they are not really doing their jobs. There is just an important balance to reach for all gymnasts and coaches, and there are thousands of brilliant gymnastics coaches in the UK who fully understand this and are amazing with it.

But - and it is a massive 'but' - if the authorities in the sport are not truly respectful of this then incidents that should never happen will take place. Coaches and administrators who overstep the mark will not be reprimanded and might even be protected, as Individual X was with me. Gymnasts and parents will feel isolated and then the integrity of the sport will be lost. Unfortunately, that is what I and hundreds of other gymnasts have felt in recent times. I lost all confidence in BG under the leadership of Jane Allen to properly care for gymnasts. That's not to say that there aren't excellent people working there but her attitude filtered down – just take Aaron Prior's attitude towards me as an example. In his first email to me, he threatened me about going public before he had even reviewed anything. I don't think he meant it as explicitly as it was received but the message was loud and clear – 'watch yourself, Nile, we can punish you'. As an opening tone, why not reassure me that I would be taken seriously and listened to? If the pressure and messaging from the top is to behave in a certain way to protect the institution, then that is what will happen eventually. Throughout my experience and that of many others, people hid behind processes. If the correct process was followed, there should be no complaints. But what is forgotten in all this is that there is a human element to this. How does your 'process' actually make young gymnasts feel? If it makes them feel unheard, isolated and 'less than', how can you, in good conscience, be satisfied with your process?

It was eye-opening to watch Jane Allen finally take on a live interview with Dan Roan and to be held accountable by his brilliant interview techniques. Her answers to his questions were shocking. He reminded Jane that she had diminished the complaint of the gymnast, Jennifer Sey, while head of gymnastics in Australia, and Jennifer had gone on to be a co-producer for the documentary *Athlete A*. Jane had no answer to it. I will never forget this question and answer, though:

Dan: You say you were confident you were in a good place, and yet we read some of the comments of some of your very top athletes. Amy Tinkler said the people running British Gymnastics, that's you, cannot be trusted. 'They've let us down. They lie,' she said. Nile Wilson, top male gymnast, told me the athletes are treated like pieces of meat. The Downie sisters spoke of cruel behaviour that was so ingrained in our daily lives, it became normalised and there was an environment of fear and abuse. These are some of your very best, most respected, most senior gymnasts. How did you not know, given their status, how unhappy they were? How can it come as such a surprise to you? Were you asleep on the job, or were you just trying to cover it up? Which of those two?

Jane: I don't think either of those. Well, I think that the organisation was working hard with its high performance programme. I think that the athletes themselves, at times, didn't speak up when they felt that way.

So was it the organisation to blame? Or that the athletes didn't speak up at the time? What about Jane taking on some genuine self-reflection that she had created a culture from top to bottom that gymnasts felt scared to make a complaint in because if they did, they would be made to feel a certain way, risk future selection and eventually not be taken seriously? And a culture that meant for some staff, they felt they must prioritise protecting the reputation of the institution?

In the same interview, Jane announced her 'retirement' only months before the independent enquiry into the sport, the Whyte Review, was due to start announcing its findings. Again, that said it all. Sadly, people like Jane Allen ruled through fear, and like all bullies, when properly confronted, she ran away.

Gymnastics has come a long way and is moving in the right direction. It is the greatest sport in the world, but it needs careful governance. If gymnasts are primarily seen as vehicle to win medals which then funds the sport, or achieve glory for parents or coaches, then there will be trouble. Gymnasts never need to be made to feel 'less than' or subservient to those above them. They will always need an outlet for their voice to be heard.

I am sure that the findings of the Whyte Review and the subsequent changes that will come from it will be positive to the sport, but why did it have to take this? We are not in 1980s' Russia and yet it took this for some action to come. The person who decided they could place their hands on me and pull me out of a social gathering is still working today in charge of coaches, gymnasts and a culture at Leeds Gymnastics Club. That should worry people, but instead they are still protected by people that look out for each other. They would rather spread false rumours about me than truly look in the mirror at what they are doing. If, one day, they are confronted in the public eye as Jane Allen was, then I am certain they would run away as she did.

I have finally found some peace with this all because I have been able to have my voice heard. Maybe not as transparently as I would like, but at least I have been able to speak my truth.

As for those in charge at Leeds Gymnastics Club – they should be ashamed of themselves.

Chapter 12

My Family

I am so lucky to be a Wilson.

I really am.

I know a lot of people say it, but my family is truly incredible. Family means so much to me and I know how lucky I am to have my parents and my sister. In fact, so much so that I want to dedicate a whole chapter to them!

Joanna's and my upbringing was amazing. I just always remember being happy. Our parents instilled so much positivity in us and there was always laughter, particularly around our dad. Our parents never 'dream bashed' us, but they made it clear to us that to achieve anything in life you needed to work hard. Most importantly, they led by example. It wasn't big lectures, it was just our way of life – without hard work, you had nothing.

A really good example of this is how they handled my gymnastics. They could see my talent and knew I could be something special but managed me brilliantly to keep me going. They didn't lecture or bully me into training; they just encouraged and allowed me to find my own way. Due to their parenting, it was in my blood to work hard and shoot for the stars. As my mum has always told Joanna and me, 'You can have it all.' I just followed their example. And I know how tough it is for gymnasts' parents. The commitment in money and time is huge and most of my earliest memories from gymnastics are being in the car with my mum. Poor Sally was basically a taxi service!

As anyone can tell from watching us on YouTube, we are a really tight unit as a family. I think this was helped by the fact that when we were kids, Dad always insisted that we have our evening meal together as a family. Taking into account that we often got back from the gym at 8.30 p.m./9.00 p.m., this meant that we usually sat down to eat at around 9.30 p.m. I know it was really late, but it meant that we had that time together as a family to talk about the day. Looking back, it was so important for us and explains so much about how we behave with each other now. We truly support each other. That might sound obvious to some of you, but the phrase doesn't quite give enough meaning to what I am trying to say. We are really intertwined in each other's lives. There is nothing that happens to any of us individually that the whole family doesn't get involved in. We are in everything together and it is a massive strength of us as a family. If you look between us now, we have multiple businesses running and we are all involved in all of them. Our passion and love for each other is really intense. That intensity and passion probably leads to us falling out once in a while, but it is only because of the strength of our love. Also, our fall-outs never last long!

It felt amazing to see my family close to me while I performed in the Olympic final. Obviously, I was trying to achieve individual success, but it was for all four of us, and when I stood on the podium crying with joy with my medal, I truly felt it for all my family. People often mention the sacrifice an athlete will have put in to achieve that moment, but the sacrifice for the family can never be underestimated. While I was training at the gym, my mum, and often Joanna, would be there too. That was four hours out of their day as well! Joanna spent many an hour doing her homework in the gym while I trained! I know everything that I have achieved and will go on to achieve, in and out of the gym, has been hugely influenced by my family, and that's why I am so grateful to them. We will always live and celebrate everything together, and I love that. And, as they mean so much to me, I would like to talk about them all individually and I'll start with Mumma Bear, Sally, Mum – or 'Sally Love' as Dad often calls her! I really do know how much my mum loves me and that is the biggest compliment I can give her.

As a little boy, and even now as a young man, you just want to know that your mum's love is always there and that has never been in doubt for me. Mum didn't know she was going to give birth to an exceptional gymnast and therefore didn't know she would spend hours and hours driving me back and forth to gymnastics training and competition. She didn't know that there would be these huge ups and downs that come with having a child who performs on the world stage. There was no preparation for this as a mother, but that didn't matter to my mum because her love and support of me has always been unconditional. Take for instance all those hours she waited for me while I trained – Mum didn't sit back and moan about it. She has been a hairdresser all her life so she filled those hours by offering to cut people's hair. Another example was at the Rio Olympics. Obtaining the tickets available for the families was a nightmare. It was badly organised and a real stress for them. So, what did Mum do? She stood in a queue to the ticketing office for two hours in the blazing heat until she could speak to someone to resolve the situation for her family. Her love and commitment to me has always been unconditional and in situations that other parents might moan about, she didn't, she made the most of it.

You have to remember that up to me being 17, Mum and I spent hours in the car together, travelling to gymnastics. She would listen to me excitedly telling her about the next thing I was going to master or achieve, or moaning about how tired, hungry and sore I was! In fact, if you added up all those hours, it would make days and days of me and Mum being with each other and chatting away. That is something I now look back on and know is really special. I had so much time and attention from my mum while I was growing up – and I know that some kids don't have that. I think it was why I would always tend to lean towards my mum rather than my dad when I was a child. Don't get me wrong though, 'our Sally' can also drive me up the wall with her nagging sometimes! But I know it is because she just wants the best for me. Even when I was about to do my retirement interview with the BBC, Mum started stressing about whether I should be cleanly shaven. Of all the things that were involved with my retirement announcement, being shaven wasn't top of the list! But Mum just wanted me to look at my best, that was it. So, I could snap at her for stressing about it, but she was only doing it for good reasons and out of love. The truth is that Mum is the heartbeat of our family. Myself, Joanna and Dad are always up to something with sport, exams, content or business; and Mum is the consistent rock that we all need. Watching her in my YouTube documentaries on my mental health battles and my retirement said it all really. She always says the same thing, that I am just 'her little boy'. And that's it, regardless of gymnastics or YouTube or business, I am just her little boy and she loves me unconditionally. That's all anyone could ask for.

OK, so on to the man, the legend, the YouTube sensation, Paps, my hero, Dad – Neil.

Many of you will have seen my dad in my YouTube videos and seen what a hilariously funny man he is – and he really is! He is the funniest person I know. So much of my childhood memories are of us laughing and a lot of that has to do with Dad. Due to his work, Joanna and I had less time with Dad so when we did have time with him, he was just determined that we would have fun. We spent hours and hours on the trampoline in the garden trying tricks and stunts or playing endless matches of cricket. It makes me laugh because Dad's garden is now his pride and joy, and as kids we just used to ruin it! Some people have said that my personality is perfect for YouTube, but that is also definitely the case with my dad. There have been so many times when I have just been about to turn on the camera and Dad has asked me what he needs to do, and I have just said 'Be funny!', and sure enough, he is!

My dad has worked hard all his life and has set an unbelievable example for work ethic for Joanna and me. Before I was 18, he was away a lot with work. In fact, he actually worked away in Glasgow for two years at one point and we didn't see him six days of the week.

That's probably why my relationship with my dad really blossomed after I turned 18. Since then we have had so much more time together, whether playing golf, making content or chatting about our gymnastics clubs, and have developed this amazing father/son or even best mates type of relationship. But probably the biggest thing that has ever happened to Dad, which affected us all, was in 2012 when he had a stroke. While he was waiting to watch me compete at the British Championships, he felt this strange sensation in his head that he describes as being like when you slightly open the top of a bottle of fizzy drink and some gas comes out. He really didn't make much of a fuss about it at the time, but eventually had it properly diagnosed and had a lengthy rehabilitation from it. The right-hand side of his body was badly affected, and he had to learn to walk without help again. It was heartbreaking and yet also inspiring to watch how Dad handled it all. But the biggest thing I would say from it is that it didn't massively change his outlook on life – his attitude and perspective on life was already brilliant before he had a stroke. This is a side of my dad that not everyone knows about. He really is an inspiring leader and so good with people. He now gives mindset talks with some of the work we are doing within our businesses and blows people away with what he says. My dad is one of the very few people I know who can mesmerise a room of people, make them laugh and make them instantly respect him. Two sayings that he always uses sum him up for me:

'It's not the thing itself, it's your attitude towards it.'
'It's 90 per cent attitude and 10 per cent fact.'

What he means by both is that we have no control over many things that happen to us in life, but we do have control of our attitude in how we react to those events or moments. So whether it was his stroke or me not performing well in a competition, it wasn't about the fact that that had happened, what mattered was how we chose to react to it. My dad didn't bemoan his stroke and has never used it as an excuse for anything. He chose to focus on how best to recover and then move forward with the life he wanted to live. That mentality has become a cornerstone of how we deal with things as a family. We accept whatever is at that moment in time and know that we then have control on how we move forward from it. That original fact of the bad thing happening can then not be used as an excuse for not getting up and moving forward again, because then you are choosing that particular attitude towards it. If, however, you choose to continue feeling sorry for yourself or moaning about something, then that's your choice.

Dad has always wanted us to embrace life at any given moment. He often said to Joanna and me, 'Go on, just show off' when we were about to perform in some way or another. He never wanted to tame our confidence or spirit. I guess it has always been his way of encouraging us to express ourselves at that particular moment. People will always see the funny side of my dad but this other side of him is incredible and has helped me so much throughout my gymnastics and my life in general.

There have been so many potentially 'viral social media moments' of my dad at gymnastics events, sometimes because he has had a few beers but mainly because he is so emotional towards anything Joanna and I do. I know the vast majority of parents are like that towards their kids but for my dad it just feels really powerful. It is not about him in the slightest, it is about how incredible he finds it to see his children living their best life. On the day of my Olympic final, Dad pretty much cried the whole day. I hadn't even competed, and he was crying. The result hadn't even happened, and he was crying. And that is because he was already incredibly proud of me. On the biggest of world stages, I was living my best life and expressing who I was with every ounce of my being. That was enough for my dad.

Last, but most definitely not least, is my sister, Joanna.

Forget that she is my sister for the time being and let me just say that Joanna is an absolutely amazing person. She is the most intelligent person I know and has a work ethic and attitude to life that would rival anyone. There are two and half years between us and she has spent so much of her life watching me training and competing and being 'Nile Wilson's sister'! But not for a moment has that stopped her going after what she wants to achieve in life. Rather than just sitting there and living off my coat tails or being envious at what I am doing, she has been just as determined to forge her own path in life. She worked incredibly hard to earn a place at Cambridge University to do the most crazily difficult science degree (when no one else from her school dreamt of doing that) and gained a 2:1. She now has multiple business interests and could basically be whatever she wants in life!

As brother and sister, we have always been very close. She says that she is my number one fan and I believe that! The pride and happiness I see in her eyes when I have done well says it all to me. I actually think Joanna has this perfect blend of my mum and dad. She can be stubborn and fiercely loyal like Mum, but also has that fun spirit of Dad. She has definitely been a daddy's girl over the years, and I can still see that now in her relationship with Dad. As close as we have always been, we didn't half fight with each other as kids as well! And I mean physically! It was just normal brother and sister stuff, but Joanna used to have this rage in her and if she got fired up enough, I knew there could be a slap coming my way! Don't worry, though, I gave it out just as much as well. Part of the problem was that if I whacked Joanna back, the rage returned, and I got another! We used to hang out a lot with our cousins, Robert and Mitchell, which meant Joanna was stuck with these three boys and was probably part of the reason for our fights. Joanna was often wrestling for survival and attention amongst us boys!

As I now grow my business interests, it is incredible to have a sister like Joanna. Not only because she is a massive supporter of mine but also because she is super intelligent and brilliant to help lead a business. I know there have been times when I have inspired Joanna but there have definitely been times when she inspires me. We are different but also the same. Her intelligence is my talent in gymnastics, but our mentalities are identical because it has been passed down to us by our parents. We both want to make the most of our lives and believe that anything is possible. I'm excited about what Joanna and I are going to achieve together and individually in the coming years.

I hope that I have given my family the words they deserve. They are so important to me and have given me so much love and support over the years. I can see the pride and happiness that I have given them when I have achieved great things in gymnastics, and I have also seen the sadness in their eyes when I have struggled with my mental health and been on a bad path. There were challenges when I moved out of the family house, started to do more things on my own and made decisions they didn't always love, but throughout it all, we have never flinched as a family. We are as tight as ever.

I am so lucky to be a Wilson.

Chapter 13

Retirement

On 14 January 2021 I announced my retirement from elite gymnastics.

I know the decision shocked some people, especially at the start of what was meant to be an Olympic year, but it had been a while in coming. Ultimately, my run of injuries had really taken their toll on me.

Since the start of 2017 my injury checklist was:

- Snapped ankle ligaments – surgery required
- Fractured foot
- Persistent nerve pain through my left hand
- Wrist ligament damage – surgery required twice
- Finger ligament damage
- Herniated disc in neck – surgery required
- Long thoracic nerve damage to right shoulder
- Another bulging disc in neck

Also, throughout this time, I had three pain-killing cortisone injections in my neck and six in my wrist.

I had always said to myself that I would retire from gymnastics when I fell out of love with it or my body couldn't take it any more. In the end, it was a bit of both, but I need to explain that in more detail.

Gymnastics is a really tough sport, which is as it should be by the way. We are throwing our bodies through the air with such pace and movement that it should be incredibly hard to do. We also do routines that can only be truly mastered with incredible repetition. So the toll on any gymnast's body is always going to be significant. The thing that many people forget, though, is that our physical fitness is not just about competing. In actual fact, competing is more of a mental thing and the physical side of it takes care of itself. Our physical fitness is about being strong enough to simply train at the level we need to. If we are physically not able to train at an elite level, then we can't even think about competing. I have heard about ageing footballers who don't train during the week due to managing injuries and then just turn up at the weekend to play in the matches. You just can't do that in gymnastics.

I battled away in training during 2020, but I could never get my body to the place it needed to be. Every time I increased my training load to get to the necessary level, my body reacted badly. I either was injured again, an old injury would flare back up, or another part of my body would get disproportionately sore. For example, my neck operation in 2019 was from the worst injury in my career and even though the neck was clinically 'fixed', the impact of the procedure and having metal in that part of my body was significant. The shoulder injury I picked up just two weeks before the World Championship trials in 2019 was due to my neck. Even now, the stability through the shoulder is still not where it needs to be and that is more than twelve months since it flared up. The problems with it are neurological as it is long thoracic nerve damage and that stems from my neck. So, although the original injury was fixed, the overall impact on my body was ongoing.

Even my neck itself flared back up. The herniated disc was fixed through surgery in February 2019, but gymnastics then put more pressure on other parts of my neck and I ended up with another bulging disc in the vertebrae above the originally damaged one. It felt as if my body was in a losing battle with gymnastics and was getting slowly, or even quickly, ground down by it. I remember speaking to the doctor after the scan revealed this second bulging disc in my neck, and genuinely having to consider whether continuing with gymnastics would risk serious long-lasting damage and therefore my ability to walk. Just that consideration in itself shows the mental challenges athletes go through when trying to weigh up whether to battle through injuries or not.

But the biggest part of my body that suffered throughout all this period, which is not on my injury check list, is my head. The mental battle in dealing with pain, rehab and then getting another injury was a cycle that began to break me. When I refer to falling out of love with gymnastics, that's the bit I am referring to, not the actual sport. I will always love gymnastics; it is the greatest sport on the earth. Gymnastics is in my blood, but I fell out of love with the process of trying to get my body to where it needed to be in order to win an Olympic gold medal. The sport that had thrilled and inspired me every day since the age of 4 and now twenty years later was starting to feel like a boring and endless walk on the treadmill. I even started to hate it at times and that was heartbreaking. Gymnastics was everything to me – my purpose, my direction and my ambition – and suddenly I started to hate it. I felt completely lost.

I have spoken in a previous chapter about how Luke and I chatted through and realised how much I attached my self-worth to how I was doing in gymnastics. It was my identity and how I felt good about myself. That's why I found being injured so tough because it was like I was half the man. I wasn't the 'Nile Wilson' that I wanted or expected of myself. And then to have this nagging doubt in the back of my mind that my body would go bust again at some point was torturous. I think, in the back of my mind, I knew my body was losing the battle in coping with the rigours of gymnastics and every time there was another injury or flare up, it sucked a bit more life out of me.

As I got to the final months of 2020, I knew it was getting to a 'make or break' moment for me over my fitness and my future in gymnastics. I needed to be in reasonable shape or at least making significant progress at the start of 2021 to be in with a realistic chance of making the Olympics. But actually, this was about more than just the Olympics. It was getting to a moment in which I would have to decide whether I still had it in me to go through what was required to be fit to be a full-time gymnast. Did I still have the resolve, the determination and resilience to overcome whatever injury was thrown at me? I chatted to my family and Luke about it a good deal during this time as it was a huge thing for all of us to contemplate. For Mum, Dad and Joanna it meant they might never get to see me perform again on the world stage; for me, I had to consider what I was going to do with the rest of my life when I had still not quite turned 25. But as 2020 came to an end and I started 2021, I knew the answer to all those questions – it was definitely time for me to retire.

One of the most difficult parts of my retirement decision was having to come to terms with what was next for me in the sport. Even though I was reaching a place where I knew I could no longer be a full-time elite gymnast, I was still deeply passionate about the sport. I didn't want to feel as though I was walking away from gymnastics, despite the fact that injuries and my fall-out with Leeds Gymnastics Club and British Gymnastics had really made me hate the sport for a while. I realised that part of my difficulty in reaching the retirement decision was that I didn't want that to be it with gymnastics, but for so long I had got used to the fact that my primary contribution to it was competing at the highest level. If I now couldn't do that, then what was my primary contribution to the sport? Because without a focus and understanding on where I fitted in with the sport, I would feel really lost.

As I talked more with my family and Luke, I started to get a vision of how I could stay an important figure within gymnastics. I could see how I could still have a focus in the sport without having to compete. As this opened up to me, it made the retirement decision more comfortable in my mind. I realised that competing was just an element of what I could offer the sport, but really what I have always wanted was to elevate gymnastics to a new place in people's interest and I could continue doing that in retirement. In fact, I might even be able to take it to another level with more time on my hands. My YouTube content has always been about making gymnastics entertaining for families so they can appreciate what a brilliant sport it is. Getting all sorts of people into the gym with me to do a back flip and have some fun on camera had always been a huge element that I brought to the sport that, respectfully, others couldn't replicate. In retirement, I would have more time to travel the world and bring my content and audience to a new level. That really excited me.

I also knew that we were creating something very special with Nile Wilson Gymnastics. Our vision and business plan for a host of gymnastics clubs around the country was incredible. The project had been hit by some of the worst initial luck with freak weather in South Yorkshire causing a huge flood at our first site, and then Covid hitting as we were about to open our second site, but our club in Rotherham was an amazing basis to start opening other clubs around the country. As I have already explained, Nile Wilson Gymnastics is focused on changing the culture in gymnastics in the UK. I could see that this was a huge thing for me to drive forward within the sport.

Finally, I could see how I could change the landscape for how gymnastics is watched by a live audience, at home on television, online or in an arena. I genuinely felt I could help shape the evolution of the sport, so it is enjoyed by a more mainstream audience. I have a clear vision of how I want to do this, which unfortunately for you, I will need to keep secret for now! Crucially, I didn't need to be competing to do this.

I have the platform, profile and ambition to do everything that I have talked about and that made me realise that I wasn't even close to finishing what I wanted to do in gymnastics. My legacy of competing might be coming to an end, but in some ways my overall contribution to the sport was only just beginning. With this clear in my mind, I knew that retiring was the right decision for me. It was the end of a chapter but the opening up of many others.

It's a strange feeling when you officially retire and start looking back on your career. You reminisce on your most in incredible moments and for me they were the 2014 and 2018 Commonwealth Games and, of course, the 2016 Rio Olympics. But you also wonder what could have been. I had focused for so many years on winning an Olympic gold medal and ultimately it didn't happen for me. Nonetheless, I know that if my body had held together, I was capable of winning the All-Around at the Tokyo Olympics. Despite my ankle injury in 2017, my scores and performances throughout 2018 were tracking in the right direction. I believed the All-Around would be won with a high 80s score, maybe 88 (Daiki Hashimoto of Japan would win with a final score of 88.465), and I had the game for that. I could perform on the High and Parallel Bars at Olympic gold medal standard; my Rings and Floor were top 6; and my Vault and Pommel Horse were good enough to hit that overall score. I also knew I had the temperament. I loved the biggest stages and thrived under that pressure. If I had to nail one routine to win then I knew I could do it.

There are some who didn't believe the Chinese can be beaten, but look what at Joe Fraser did at the 2019 World Championships in the Parallel Bars. As others made mistakes under pressure, he held his nerve and came away with the gold. Those big competitions are mainly about your temperament under the highest pressure. Do you suffocate under the fear of what mistake you might make? Or thrive with the opportunity you can see ahead of you? I was never driven by fear and it's why I so often competed with a massive smile on my face! I could visualise how cool it would look when I nailed my routine! I know that if I had got through 2019 and 2020 relatively injury free then an Olympic gold medal was a realistic goal for me.

It wasn't to be, though, but I don't hold any sort of regret or resentment about that. I am truly grateful for what I was able to achieve in gymnastics. I have always said that I want to 'change the game' in gymnastics and I feel I did and am still doing that. Great Britain's first ever Olympic medal in the High Bar will move the dial for that apparatus, as Louis Smith did with his bronze medal at the 2008 Beijing Olympics. Other gymnasts will see what is possible and will surpass that achievement one day, as Max Whitlock did with Louis. Being the most successful ever British gymnast at the Commonwealth Games will stay in the history books for some time as well. Even being the most successful junior British gymnast at a European Championships sits proudly in my achievements. Whether a junior or senior, I would like other gymnasts now to aim for some of my achievements and surpass them so we can keep this amazing sport moving forward in the United Kingdom.

The point is that my performances made an impact in the sport and that's what matters to me. There might always have been something more I could have won in gymnastics, even if I had stayed injury free, but the fact that what I did achieve will always be remembered sits well with me.

I also know that I have been part of some great British Gymnastics Men's teams. To have competed alongside the guys and won medals has been a massive pleasure. I felt part of something truly powerful and special. I thrived in the team competitions and that was because I felt such a close bond with the other guys in the team. There were the superstars like Louis and Max, but more than anything, we were a team in which everyone was equally important. We were trying to achieve things in the sport that had not yet been done and it was an honour to be part of that sense of purpose and meaning. Looking back, our build-up as a team to the Rio Olympics was incredible. Our silver medal in the Team All-Around at the 2015 World Championships in Glasgow, when I was just 19, will live with me forever. We were such a close unit and inspired each other to push the boundaries of what people believed was possible. We were proving that British gymnastics was here to stay at the highest level of world gymnastics alongside the giants of China, Russia and Japan. I know the likes of Joe Fraser and Courtney Tulloch will proudly carry that torch for us going forward. Those team events and medals were extremely special for me.

More than anything else, though, I have always wanted to put a spotlight on gymnastics. I have wanted to broaden the horizons of the sport – to get people interested in it that ordinarily wouldn't be. I have wanted to make people smile and be entertained when they watch and learn about the sport. I have wanted to inspire millions of children to take part and for parents to see it as something brilliant for their child to be involved in. I have wanted to bring character and style to the sport. Through my achievements, the style I have performed in and all the content I have produced online, I feel as though I have been doing that. The hundreds of thousands of letters and messages that I have received over the years have shown me that. The enormous queues of people at major events waiting for my and my family's autographs have shown me that. The roars of the crowds I have received wherever I have competed have shown me that. The overall reaction to what I have always been trying to do has been phenomenal. Even to this day, I get messages from people telling me about how my journey in the sport helped them through school or university in dealing with difficulty or adversity in some way or another. There is no medal that can match how much that means to me. To be able to help inspire people through their lives is the proudest part of anything I have or will ever achieve.

So, I didn't retire from elite gymnastics harbouring any phrases beginning with 'I could've' or 'I should've'. I am at peace with the decision and know that I am not even close to being finished in the sport, even if the competing part of it has ended.

I am truly grateful for everything my gymnastics career brought me.

Chapter 14

Business

I started looking into wealth creation when I was just 17 years old. This was well before any Olympics Games, World Championships or explosion on YouTube – I was immediately fascinated by it.

I read books like *Rich Dad Poor Dad* and *Secrets of a Millionaire Mind* and knew straight away that I didn't want to be constrained by anything society might tell me. Not that there is anything wrong with this, but I didn't just want to go to school, get a job and retire. I wanted more. I didn't want boundaries like that in my mind and, even at that age, was positioning myself to understand how to create wealth.

Then, as I was creating content online in late 2016/early 2017, Gary Vaynerchuk or 'Gary Vee' as he is better known, became a massive influence on me. I loved how he encouraged you to live life as a good human being, with empathy and purpose, but more than anything he showed me what was possible with using content to market yourself online. I could see that I could create successful businesses that I marketed through incredible content on my social media and YouTube channel. Gary was a massive inspiration for everything you see me doing nowadays.

Gary did eventually say in one of his videos 'Stop watching my shit and go out there and do it!' and he was right, so I went out there and did it!

Amazing content drives everything and from it so many business opportunities can be created and thrive. I think a lot of people get this the wrong way around with content. They start businesses and then think about what content can be created to help market it. With whatever business idea my team and I are thinking through, I begin by considering how I could create content for it because I know that incredible content will make people notice it. Unfortunately, you can have the best business idea in the world but if no one knows about it then you're knackered.

There have been so many challenger brands that have taken on the big boys by using the power of online content and reach. I'm proud to be a Gymshark ambassador and to see what they have done within the sportswear industry is incredible. No one would have given them a chance in taking on the likes of adidas and Nike; in fact, they were described to me more as a 'marketing' company a few years ago. But those people couldn't see how brilliant Gymshark were. They were producing great products but more than anything they were producing amazing content via social media. It became a massive marketing tool for them. Before the giants could see it happening, Gymshark were catching up and then matching them. When I signed with the company at the start of 2021, it really felt like a perfect match. Both of us truly understood the power of creating breathtaking content to reach millions and millions of people without having to use TV or Radio advertising.

I am now fortunate to be a business owner of multiple companies and I think every one of them has been born in some way or another from my social media and YouTube channels. That might sound strange when you think about the gymnastics clubs we own as they are physical sites for gymnasts to come to, but what gives us the confidence to invest and go for these opportunities is that I am able to market them through my platforms. We bought Rotherham Gymnastics Club in 2019 and had to move to a new site 25 miles away due to a flood. We had a brand new 10,000 square foot facility which was amazing but also needed filling! Some of the membership from our old site came with us but being a reasonable distance apart meant that not everyone was able to do so. The reality is that the move presented a big risk for us, but we had confidence that we could make it work by marketing it through my content – and that is exactly what we were able to do. It is a really good example of how a business opportunity was brought to reality because of the platform my content had created.

I am definitely an entrepreneur at heart. I love hearing about new ideas and challenging myself to think outside the box. Luke has described managing me as trying to keep up with a runaway train at times and I totally understand that. I feel as if I can take on the world and that truly anything is possible; that challenge of taking something from an idea to reality gives me a massive buzz. Wrapped into that is that I don't fear failure in business, in exactly the same way that I didn't fear failure with my gymnastics. My team and I have had a lot of brilliant days in business, but we have also made a lot of mistakes. It does not mean that we were 'failing' when we were making those mistakes, though. In fact, every mistake has just been a step closer to us getting it right. I always use this phrase to remind myself and others about this point: 'No one ever succeeded their way to success.' Mistakes are part of a natural process in eventually getting it right. As long as you have good people around you and are determined not to give up, then anything is possible.

My first business venture was the Body Bible – a website that sold gymnastics-based training programmes. I worked with two of my coaches, Dave Murray and Tom Rawlinson, to create various programmes that would help people improve their physical condition, whatever level they were at, by using gymnastics. As ever, I used my social media and YouTube to help promote the Body Bible. I knew immediately what sort of content I could create to market the programmes that would engage people. It was a massive success and we were able to build a huge community of people using the programmes and gaining benefit from them. I know how incredible gymnastics is for your body and to be able to bring training programmes to a mainstream audience was amazing. Importantly, as a business, it was very efficient. There was a lot of hard work in creating the programmes and the videos to go with them but once that was done, everything else was relatively cost effective to manage. I was to go on to bigger business ideas than the Body Bible, but as a first venture it was a perfect example of everything I had learnt from, and been inspired by, Gary Vee. I was able to bring alive a product online by amplifying it through my social media. It was only the start for me with business, but it proved what my team and I were capable of.

From there, I knew that so much more could be created from my online marketing power. I was injured for the 2017 British Championships, so we decided to get 300 T-shirts with 'Train Smart, Keep It Real' printed on them to sell at a stall in the arena. I promoted that this was happening on my social media channels and the result was crazy! There were queues all round the arena as people sacrificed missing the live gymnastics to come and buy one of my T-shirts from me. The demand for the T-shirts was incredible and we made £5,000 from sales on the day. We suddenly realised there was a huge merchandise opportunity. 'NW Clothing' was created, and it just exploded! We were producing items like hoodies, T-shirts, shorts, caps, water bottles and phone cases and the sales were excellent. I remember being on holiday after the 2018 Commonwealth Games and we launched a new drop of the merchandise. Luke, Joanna and I were watching the back-end system to see what would happen when we went live; well … we sold over £50,000 worth of items within twenty-four hours. It was insane! There was just this huge enthusiasm for merchandise based around me and we had this massive online marketing machine to drive it all forward. It was an incredibly unusual position to be in as an athlete because normally you are desperately looking for a sportswear sponsorship from a company like adidas or Nike, but for me, I had this merchandise sales arm to what I did that dwarfed most of these sorts of deals. I actually signed with adidas in 2018 and part of the negotiation was ensuring that I could still run my merchandise company. In truth, if I couldn't then the deal wouldn't have been worth me taking up, which is mad to think as a 23-year-old athlete at the time.

My passion in business has always been so strong. I have watched athletes like Conor McGregor in awe. Yes, as a fighter he is immense, but also as a businessman. He never just sat back and collected his fight pay cheques; he wanted more. More challenge and, obviously, more money. I could see how Conor used his profile to generate multiple business interests. I massively admire his vision and tenacity for all this because the thing that every athlete faces when you start to do things outside of your sport is someone saying, 'shouldn't you just be concentrating on your training'. That happened to me constantly as people questioned my commitment and focus. But it was never like that for me; my outside interests never distracted me from my gymnastics, and I presume it was the same for Conor as well. If all I ever did in life was gymnastics – train, sleep, eat and repeat – I would go mad. I would get bored with it all. I needed things outside of the sport to inspire and challenge me; it would actually make me a better version of myself in the gym. I know that's not the same for other athletes and Max Whitlock, for example, leads a much quieter and simpler life as a gymnast because that's what was right for him. We are just very different people and therefore had different ways we wanted to go about our careers. Ultimately, it is what works for you; for me, I need business ventures outside of gymnastics.

I am fortunate to have collaborated with some massive global companies over the years like Sony and Coca Cola. I see those collaborations as part of my business interests. They are not stand-alone company set ups, but I see them as joint ventures in my mind for particular campaigns. As ever, they are driven by my content. If my content is dynamic and engaging, then those companies will want to partner with it to bring to life a new product they want to advertise. Creating this sort of content is not easy, though; I can't just make it up on the spot. It takes planning, briefing sessions, filming and then a lot of post-production work. I use a team of various cameramen, sound engineers and video editors when doing all of this. We are basically a production team in which I am the director and the star of the show. My point with all this is that my approach to these sorts of collaborations is different from 99.9 per cent of other high-profile sportspeople. They see themselves solely as the 'face' that the company wants to use and nothing much more to it than that. So they are in and out of the job relatively quickly. Whereas I see it as much more than that. There will always be someone more famous than you and eventually your star will fade. If you see these sorts of collaborations as being 'the face', you have to accept that eventually they will die away. I was collaborating with the likes of Sony and Coca Cola when there were much more famous athletes than me, but I was able to bring to the table things that they couldn't. Firstly, I could take away a massive headache for the brand by creating brilliant content rather than waiting for them to do it. And secondly, I also had an online platform I could use to amplify the collaboration to an enormous reach. These things did not depend on whether I won an Olympic gold or not. I see this area of my life as a business, a version of a production company, even though strictly speaking it isn't a limited company. With this approach, and as long as I am creating brilliant content that is reaching millions of people, then I will always have strong commercial worth.

I think the most significant step into business I made in the last couple of years was with Nile Wilson Gymnastics. We are told that there are somewhere between 1 and 2 million children on gymnastics club waiting lists around the UK, which breaks my heart to hear. The grassroots interest in our sport is enormous and yet we just don't have enough facilities for them to come to. That is just not good enough, in my opinion. We have the greatest sport in the world and we should be doing everything we can to get as many kids taking part in it as possible. Regardless of this, though, I have felt for a long time that the gymnastics club industry needed something new and different. Although there are some good gymnastics clubs in the UK, the general experience for families is pretty poor. This can be from a spectator point of view, with inadequate viewing areas and makeshift cafes, but also on a deeper level. I have spoken about this in the press but the urgency to create elite gymnasts as quickly as possible has caused a real downside to the experience people feel at some clubs. Children who are not quite good enough soon feel alienated and the sense of fun gets lost too quickly. There is too much focus on the actual gymnastics and not enough on the general development of kids – how they interact, how they build confidence and how they have fun! I was fortunate to be blessed with a mind and body that was ready for elite gymnastics, but it doesn't mean that someone who doesn't have that has any less right to enjoy gymnastics the way I have. For a long time, there has been a danger in gymnastics that the sport is being driven by coaches searching for credibility that they can produce a star gymnast. The sport can't be dominated in that way. We will always have space for elite pathways to produce the next Nile Wilson, but we have a greater responsibility than that. All children who leave a gymnastics club should do so with smiles on their faces after they have just taken part in something that has been fun, amazing and helped them develop. Entire families should be benefiting from their experience at a gymnastics club but, unfortunately, that is being lost far too often. We wanted to change all of this. In fact, we wanted to go about 'Changing the Game' in this whole area.

My dad and I had talked for a long time about opening up our own chain of gymnastics clubs, especially after a glass or two of red wine! But as things developed with Luke and a couple of other investors, we started to make this a reality. We had a strong group of people involved with a brilliant vision and decent amounts of available investment, but we just needed to find our first club. This would either be a brand-new site, or we would acquire an existing club. My poor dad most have spent a year on the search for our first step into the market without any luck! It was a nightmare trying to find somewhere but eventually we came across Rotherham Gymnastics Club. It was a decent club, about ten years old, and crucially the owners wanted to sell. The club needed some work on it in a lot of different ways, but it represented a start in the market for us. After the normal back and forth of negotiations, we eventually got to an agreement and took over the club in September 2019. It was a massive moment for all of us! My dad had worked so hard in trying to find a club for us to start at and it was another one of these big ideas that we had actually made reality. One of the cornerstones of my mindset and that of my family and my team is that anything is possible. If someone had said that a 23-year-old gymnast would start a chain of gymnastics clubs then someone else might laugh. But not for us – we made it real!

Rotherham was a start for us and was a very different business from others I had set up previously. Yes, I could drive interest to it via my online platform, but there was a whole business of people that needed managing on a day-to-day basis. My dad, with Luke, led that incredibly well and it has been an eye-opener for me. All my online businesses have been very cost effective and that's why they can be so profitable, but for the club there were massive overheads in running a 10,000 square foot facility. I started to learn so much about how we could drive forward this sort of business. We knew we could implement some changes to the club that could massively alter the experience for families. Those first six weeks were absolutely relentless, especially for my mum and dad who were managing the club 24/7, but we were making serious progress. The number of gymnasts coming through the door was increasing every week but more importantly, the experience for them and their parents was changing. People left the building with smiles on their faces and that was what it was all about for us.

Then came the freak weather in South Yorkshire at the start of November 2019! I think there was something like three months rainfall in seventy-two hours and our gym was right at the bottom of some hills in the town. The club had never been a flood risk previously, but it was just the sheer weight of rain in such a short period of time that caused a massive problem: the gym flooded. It was heartbreaking!

Especially for my dad, who was at the gym as the water started to break through, and had been the heart and soul of everything that was happening there. It felt as though all that hard work was being trashed as the interior of the gym was ruined. We had ankle/shin-high water throughout the building, which ruined carpets and vast amounts of equipment. We shared photos and videos on social media to show people the extent of the damage.

But, as ever, we didn't give up! With the support of all the coaches and many parents, we began a massive clearing-up exercise of the gym. This was a big blow to what we had been doing, but there wasn't a moment when we didn't believe we would make our way through this. Our mindset was again the absolute key. Our intentions were always to continue at that site in Rotherham, but unfortunately, once it had been flooded like that the insurance implications changed completely and we could not get the necessary insurance in place. My dad had searched for twelve months to find this site, however, the reality was that we were going to need to move. Fortunately for us, our landlord owned multiple bits of land that he built huge warehouse type facilities on, and mentioned that he had another possible site for us about 10 to 15 miles away in Dinnington. We visited it and it was perfect. In fact a huge improvement on the site at Rotherham. This was obviously great, but we had invested so much money and time into Rotherham and we would be starting all over again in so many ways at Dinnington. It was a huge challenge.

I have carried my mindset from my gymnastics into business and surrounded myself with people who think the same way. In the face of problems or challenges, we find a way to make it work. We never give up and we always support each other. That is what we did in making it work at Dinnington. We now have an incredible facility, and the heartbreak of the floods seems miles away. Unfortunately, Nile Wilson Gymnastics at Dinnington was then hit by Covid! We have faced the same challenges as millions of other businesses throughout an incredibly difficult time, but you know what, we have made it work, again! Once Covid is long gone we will have a gymnastics club at Dinnington which is special in every way and by the time you read this, we might have even opened our second club. This is just the start for us with Nile Wilson Gymnastics and I am incredibly excited about what we can do in the next few years.

My passion for business has given me so much. Yes, financially it has moved me to another level, but it has also given me a place to put my focus and energy away from my actual gymnastics. I am in no doubt that my retirement announcement would have been infinitely harder if I didn't have all these other things going on. At retirement, every athlete asks the question 'What now?' and for me that was easily answered. There is so much more I want and believe I can achieve in business. It gives me the same buzz as when I did something special inside a gymnastics arena, and I am going to go for it!

Chapter 15

Gymnastics Coaching

During my interview with Dan Roan from the BBC in August 2020, I described a 'culture of abuse' in gymnastics.

It was a comment that rightly drew a lot of attention. I had highlighted an uncomfortable truth that some in gymnastics wanted to be said and some desperately didn't want to hear. This chapter is an opportunity for me to add more context around this comment and how I see the future of gymnastics coaching around the world. In doing this, I am going to highlight the three coaches who had the most influence on me throughout my career.

The first thing I need to say is that I entirely stand by that comment I made last year, and I am so glad I had the platform to do so.

I have briefly mentioned the environment that I grew up in as a gymnast in Leeds earlier in this book – it was genuinely scary at times. If you wanted to be a gymnast, especially an elite one, then you were put through pain, both emotional and physical. It is an incredibly tough sport and the mentality amongst coaches back then was that this was required in order to get people up to standard. Coaching was very consequence driven – if you performed a skill badly, you would be punished for it. Being shouted at or mocked was fairly routine, and the physical punishment was pretty brutal at times. Would you describe this as 'abuse'? Yes, I believe you would. The question I ask myself now is would I let my son or daughter go through that and the answer is absolutely not.

This environment was just the way it was. Parents knew how hard it was but were also placed in a position to believe that if they wanted their son or daughter to do well in gymnastics then they would need to go through this. I believe this came from the influence of us watching Russian gymnasts dominate world gymnastics and being told that their coaching was a fundamental reason behind this, and guess what – their coaching methods were extremely strict and brutal. And this feels strange to say but I don't doubt that my upbringing in gymnastics helped me eventually reach the top. I was forced to become incredibly resilient both mentally and physically from a young age, but please don't mistake this as me meaning that I believe this was the only way for me to reach the top. In fact, my experiences when I moved from junior to senior elite level gymnastics proved the point that we didn't need that brutal environment to excel. I will come back to this point.

So why was there this intensity around producing top gymnasts and therefore trying to replicate the Russian model for coaching? The answer has been a fundamental flaw in our sport for far too long. The vast majority of coaches back then, and some today, see the gymnast as being the means to them being recognised as a top coach. It is almost like a father living his sporting dreams through his talented son or daughter and is actually more about their perceived glory than anything else. For those same coaches, the recognition of success was purely medals. If your gymnast was winning lots of medals, then you would be seen as a great coach and move forward within the sport. This produced an environment where coaching was focused on the few and not the many. Some coaches were looking for the next Nile Wilson and would sift out the weak from the strong. They made the environment so tough that anyone not capable of surviving in it walked away, and they didn't care about that. The number of times I have heard stories of coaches, even in recent times, saying to a parent 'Well, your child is just not strong enough for gymnastics' is shocking. Please be in no doubt that this mentality is alive and kicking in many parts of grassroots gymnastics coaching today. Yes, I survived this environment, but I was gifted. What happens to the kids that aren't that gifted? Their confidence is shattered, and then they are told to go away as they are 'not strong enough' for the sport.

Even worse, what happens to the kids who hang in there for years and years with the sport but are never quite good enough? The ones who are berated for years without ever quite satisfying their coach's brutal demands. Their self-esteem is gradually eroded until eventually they have to leave the sport because of how fundamentally unhappy they are. Is anyone seriously trying to justify this?

My first hugely influential coach was Moussa Hamani or 'Zah' as we nicknamed him. Moussa is a French Algerian and as tough as they came as a coach. He was my head coach at Leeds Gymnastics Club from about 5 to 15 years old and was a great influence on me. I was genuinely scared of him at times, but he taught me discipline and pushed me to be the best I could be. He definitely saw me as a potential star, and I was seen by others as being his 'golden boy'. As a result, he gave me a huge amount of attention as he saw me as his personal project. In fact, so much so that he clashed a lot with my junior national coach, Baz Collie. I will never forget one incident in the gym when I was around 11 and Baz had been in the gym with me. Baz wanted me to do a skill called an 'Invert Giant' in a particular way, which happened to be different from the way Moussa wanted me to do it. As I was practising it, Moussa stormed over and demanded to know why I was doing the skill that way. I told him that Baz wanted me to do it that way and Moussa screamed back 'Well, I never want to coach you again!'

I was upset, grabbed my stuff and stormed out of the gym! I went to see my mum and dad in the viewing area and cried my eyes out. I was just doing what I was told and stuck in between two coaches battling for supremacy. My parents persuaded me back into the gym and I ended being some sort of mediator between Moussa and Baz! I actually think Moussa agreed with Baz but just didn't want to be seen to be junior to Baz as my coach.

Moussa was hard work at times and you never quite knew what you would be walking into at the gym with him, but he demanded the best from me, and that drove me forward. As I received my Olympic medal, there were fundamentals that Moussa had coached into me that were a part of me achieving that medal. But there is no doubt that the coaching environment back then was a very tough one. Coaches believed that was the only way to produce elite gymnasts and their methods and styles understandably upset a lot of children and parents. I survived that type of coaching and, in the end, benefited from it, but I was perceived as a future star. What happened to all the other gymnasts who couldn't come through that or weren't given the attention I was given? The reality is that they would have walked away disillusioned or heartbroken. Gymnastics failed back then, and sadly still does at times, to recognise that their right to enjoy the best sport in the world is as important as someone as gifted as me. Yes, we have moved away from this in recent years but nowhere near as much as some people want to tell themselves.

My deep frustration and even anger towards the likes of Jane Allen and Individual X at Leeds Gymnastics Club stems from this. In the same interview with Dan Roan, I described gymnasts as being treated like 'pieces of meat' and that is true. From the top level to the grassroots level, there still exists an attitude amongst some that a brilliant gymnast will win medals and that will give everyone, from coach to administrator to chief executive, the credibility that they all so crave. This then creates an environment where genuine care for the gymnast is not considered anywhere near enough. The focus will be on the few and not the many, and even those few will be pushed to their limits and beyond. You then add in another layer to this that if anyone ever complains about it, they will be silenced in order not to damage the reputation of the institution; because those people craving glory off the back of gymnasts need their power within the institution to remain. This dynamic was amplified by a UK Sport model that granted money to sports for the medals they won. People have been playing with young people's lives in a bid for their own glory and everything that comes with it, including money. It makes me so happy to think that I might have had a role in helping this

dynamic be corrected within our sport. Progress has been made in
the sport since I was 10 years old but there is still a long way to go.
I urge you to be wary of anyone within gymnastics that tells you this is
not true. Ask yourself, why are they so scared of admitting that more
progress needs to be made?

As I document all of this, it is so important for me to add that
I have been blessed to work with some of the best coaches out there;
ones who don't fall in line with this mentality at all. The first I want
to talk about is Baz Collie. Baz started coaching me when I was about
9 years old and was my junior national coach and then joined me
with the senior set up. I have had and still have an incredibly close
relationship with Baz – he is a brilliant man. I know no better coach to
inspire you and he could light me up in the gym whether I was as fresh
as a daisy or exhausted after my sixth straight day of hard and long
training. I always wanted to impress Baz. Technically he is a 10 out
of 10 coach, but more than anything was how he connected with me
on an emotional level. The connection was and still is huge with Baz.
When I felt that he was with me on my journey as a gymnast, it was
really intense. I knew he was living and breathing every second of my
development and performance. That is why when we had that five-
minute phone call before I collected my Olympic medal, it was so
emotional – Baz had walked the entire journey with me. As with any
emotional relationship, there was also the odd fall-out between us. It
was just the intensity of our relationship bubbled over. If we didn't
feel the other one was giving what we expected in the partnership,
then it kicked off! But we actually grew out of those moments and
our bond became stronger. I owe Baz, along with Dave Murray, so
much for what I achieved in gymnastics. British Gymnastics is lucky
to have Baz and I know he will be giving that same energy he gave to
me to others now.

The other most influential coach in my career was Dave Murray.
Dave was the lead elite coach at Leeds Gymnastics Club and someone
whom I had training alongside when I was younger. I don't know

anyone more dedicated and passionate about gymnastics than Dave. He is a lovely man and as a coach was completely committed to me. In fact, Dave is the absolute opposite of the coaches I have described who chase personal recognition through their gymnasts. The truth is that if Dave pushed himself further forward then he would be far more recognised for his work, but he has always seemed to be happy under the radar. There is no ego or agenda with Dave, he just wanted to do the best job he could and for me to be the best gymnast I could be. A big part of my heartbreak in being forced to leave Leeds Gymnastics Club was not being able to work with Dave consistently any more. I may have always had a more openly emotional relationship with Baz, but the depth of my admiration and love for Dave was no different.

The contrast between Dave and Baz as personalities couldn't have been greater but it meant that the blend of them worked brilliantly for me. I got the best of both worlds – if Baz was the coach to light me up, Dave was the one to keep me grounded. In fact, Dave was so grounding and understated that it became a running joke. His phrase 'it's getting there' was famous amongst us all. I could perform the greatest routine ever seen in the history of gymnastics, causing Baz to run around the gym naked in celebration, and Dave's response would be 'it's getting there'. After my retirement, Dave wrote me a really long and emotional message, which was truly amazing and at the bottom of the message it said: 'It's getting there.'

Looking back now, I can see that in some ways I have a similar personality to Baz, so we were electric together, but I also need grounding once in a while and Dave did that for me. I was really lucky to work with both of them, as will be other gymnasts in the future.

Where does gymnastics coaching go from here?

As I write this, seventeen former gymnasts, including three Olympians, are taking legal action against British Gymnastics over what they say was systemic physical and psychological abuse in the sport; and possibly by the time you read this, the Whyte Review will have presented its findings on the sport's handling of issues around gymnasts' welfare. Whatever the findings are, there is clearly a demand for a change in the sport. We will never know the true cost of some of the coaching methods and attitudes that have existed in our sport because they can show themselves in subtle ways. Crushing someone's self-esteem or self-worth at a young age can cause mental health issues that plague someone for years without it being totally obvious to the outside world.

Now is the time for change and I want to take some responsibility for that.

Speaking up publicly was a first step, but what I can do with our Nile Wilson Gymnastics clubs all around the UK and the world for children and adults can be a far greater movement. I want all children and parents who visit one of our gymnastics clubs to leave with smiles on their faces. Smiles that are a result of fun experiences that have helped grow self-confidence whatever ability people have. Of course, it would be wonderful if we could bring through an Olympian, but it is equally vital that we provide an experience within our sport that makes everyone feel valued and important. Gymnastics is the greatest sport in the world, and it is a travesty that there has been so much heartbreak caused by coaches or administrators within the sport who have felt it was all about them. That will never happen at one of my gymnastics clubs.

Gymnastics is an incredibly physical sport. Physiologically speaking, gymnasts are some of the most well-balanced athletes in the world. We have lifted, twisted and thrown ourselves in so many different ways so that our bodies can be perfectly in tune. We are the closest to human beings trying to fly at times and it is amazing! People watch our sport in awe at what we can do and that is the reason why I never have an issue trying to find people from other walks of life to come try a back flip with me for my YouTube channel. But, and it is a big 'but', it is now time for the sport to be an incredible experience for people's minds as well as their bodies. The sport can create incredible athletes, but I want it now to be renowned for how it creates an incredible mindset for anyone that tries it. Not a mindset created from surviving a bullying environment, but a mindset that fears nothing and believes everything is possible. One that holds a person in good stead whether they become an Olympian or not.

Our sport is blessed with a massive grassroots demand. As I have already said in this book, it is a tragedy that there are over a million children on waiting lists to join a gymnastics club. But the statistic that is often overlooked within the sport is the dropout rate – children who start it and then stop for one reason or another. Too many children give up the sport because it is not fun for them any more and that has to change. Coaching that creates a conflict between progression and fun is not the coaching I want in the sport. Children will all progress at different levels, but they must all have fun in the process.

We have the greatest sport in the world, but it must be treated carefully by good people and we must all do our bit to set a good example. In retirement, this will be a massive focus of mine.

Chapter 16

The Future of Our Sport

People have always been captivated when watching gymnastics. We can do things with our bodies that other people find astonishing. Someone once described gymnastics to me as watching superhumans showing off and I completely understand that. There is such an incredible blend in our sport of beauty, grace, power, balance and explosion that makes it like no other out there. This is why there has always been an opportunity to create great online content around gymnastics. As I have grown in followers, subscribers and viewers, people have continually asked me how I do it – 'what is the secret behind it all?' Well, the truth is that it is like many successful things in life – it looks easy but is actually extremely difficult. My content has evolved since I was 14 years old and for every viral video that I have produced, there have been at least ten that didn't go anywhere near as far. Through all this time, I have been a student of what makes great content, and I can tell you that gymnastics being amazing has never been enough.

Don't get me wrong, trying to create fun content as a gymnast is a hell of a lot easier than if I did crown bowls for a living, but there has always needed to be more depth to my content. The reality is that as an elite gymnast, I was training about four to six hours a day for six days of the week – it is not actually that exciting! Over time I worked out that the amazingness of gymnastics needed to be the icing on the cake for my content, not the base of it. If it was just as simple as putting gymnastics on to YouTube, then anyone could do it or maybe just the most famous gymnast in the world would be the best at it. You could then actually say the same for any other sport on YouTube, it would just be a battle of who was the most famous. But it doesn't work like that, which is why many of the emerging YouTubers are people that the mainstream audiences have never heard of. As I became more experienced with my content, I realised that I needed to entertain people. Many people face struggles in their life so when they clicked on to watch my video and gave up ten minutes of their life to me, I knew that I needed to make them smile and laugh, at the very least.

Naturally, I have always been the type of personality that enjoys entertaining people anyway. I love to perform in an arena in front of thousands of people and I'm not exactly shy! But 'entertainment' is about a lot more than just telling jokes and falling over. I always had a sense that in order to truly entertain viewers, I needed to connect with them – or rather they needed to connect with me. And to do that, I needed to 'let them in' to who I was and the life I led. I needed to tell people how I was feeling, whether it was a good day or a bad day. I wanted people watching to feel as though they really knew me. If there was that authenticity to my content then people would feel they were on my journey with me and we could all laugh, cry, and everything in between, together. That is why it was natural for me to introduce my family to my audience; it was just letting people see more of my life. I am so lucky that my family are incredibly entertaining in themselves and are always so willing to be part of it. My dad has always been a centre point for the entertainment with my family and he is an absolute legend! Our 'Neil and Nile Vlogs' became so popular in a short period of time as people loved our father/son relationship and how funny my dad is. But my mum and Joanna have found their place within it all, and people watching love them as well.

The one thing I didn't realise that would come along with all of my content, though, was how much I would inspire people. Over the last few years, I have received tens of thousands of messages from people sharing how much they have got from my content on a personal level. How it has inspired them to get through a difficult spell in their life or overcome a challenge they never thought they could.

This might sound strange to people but this part of it caught me by surprise. I just wanted to create eye-catching and entertaining content but suddenly it seemed I was creating this movement that people were drawing inspiration from. It blew my mind a bit and still does in some ways. What I have discovered over time is that without realising it, I was opening people up to the mindset that I live by. This is the mindset that my parents conditioned in me as a young boy and that other key people in my life have encouraged and even amplified further. The truth is that it was the mindset that took me to becoming an Olympic medallist.

My parents never put boundaries on my dreams. As I have already said, my mum has always said to Joanna and me 'You can have it all', meaning that the world is our oyster. We can go out into the world and achieve what we want. We can make what seems an impossibility become a reality. We knew that needed to be matched with hard work and commitment, but we have lived and breathed an attitude of 'we can do this!' That is reflected not just in my achievements but Joanna's as well. I am so grateful that my parents have been that influence on us and shown us a way to approach life that has always seem so natural to us. As I let people into my personality and life online, they got a glimpse of that mindset and that's what inspired people. Even when I had my major ankle surgery in 2017 and faced a long time out of gymnastics, I still had the same mindset I had the year before when I was smashing it in the Olympics. I was looking forward and knew that I would come back from it even stronger than before. This is another reason why my growth in YouTube through 2017 was nothing to do with my profile or fame, it was because people were hooking on to the journey and the mindset I had.

The biggest influence on my mindset, outside of my parents, is most definitely Michael Finnigan. Michael has been a massive part of everything I have managed to achieve in and out of the gym. I was first introduced to Michael by my dad before the Rio Olympics. My dad used to work at The Direct Line Group and Michael had been brought in to run mindset sessions with some of the company's main leaders, including my dad. The programme, conceived and written by Michael himself, was called 'Impossible to Inevitable' or 'i2i'. My dad was blown away by it and wanted me to meet Michael. We hit it off immediately and he is an amazing man. I loved everything that Michael was about, and I think he could see in me someone that already had much of what he was trying to teach in people. The biggest thing that Michael instilled in me was that I had the power to go out there and achieve greatness whether it was in the gym or elsewhere – I could make the impossible inevitable. I already had access to everything I needed within me, it was all about mindset. That would drive my behaviours and my behaviours would drive my outcomes. There was no fear involved and all I would see ahead of me was opportunity. Everything was within my grasp.

Prior to the Rio Olympics, Michael and I met for long chats and I always got so much from them. We didn't formally do the i2i programme, but we talked its language and Michael gave me so much insight. It is where my 'Inevitable Dream' came from that became reality in my Olympic final. It was actually post Rio that Michael and I worked closer together, and I then did the full programme with him. He lives near Bolton and we met up on the M62 services for an hour or two at a time. During a difficult period of time for me and my recovery from my ankle surgery, this was just brilliant for me. This mindset work with Michael was invaluable; I was moving forward as a person and I guess this came shining through in the content I was putting out there online.

Over the last four or five years, Michael has been a mentor that I could always go to and he would realign so much of my thinking. He really helped me when I was considering retirement because it was such a huge thing to contemplate. For any athlete, retirement can bring up a lot of fear around finding a way to live your life without the very thing that *is* your life. His approach with this, as with everything else, was to look at the opportunities available to me rather than being driven by fear. Fear can be an obstacle in all our lives that traps us into believing that we don't have the power to create the path we want to in life. The 'what ifs' can cripple our thought processes. Michael is exceptional at helping me see beyond that. He actually makes everything seem so much simpler. The 'what ifs' become 'why nots' and the impossible becomes the inevitable. Even though I might not have realised it from the start, my attitude and approach to life has always been something that people have connected with. I am grateful for the likes of Michael Finnigan, who helped that mindset shine through as it not only helped me as an athlete but also beyond the gym with my content and then the businesses that grew from it. Michael once asked me to write a 'Life List', which is a bit like a Bucket List but without the death element involved! I wrote a list of about fifty things and put it away in a cupboard. Only recently did I find that list and that were some bold aims on there when I wrote it – but even more incredible was that fact that almost all of them had now become reality.

As I always say, gymnastics is the greatest sport on the planet, and I want as many people as possible to enjoy it. In the end, I have always wanted my content to attract people to watch the sport whether they were experts or knew nothing about gymnastics. I wanted there to be something for everyone in it. If you were an aspiring gymnast then you could watch my skills and training and learn a lot from it; if you were a casual observer, you could be amazed by the sport but also have a bloody good laugh! Despite it being online, I have always been about trying to make gymnastics more mainstream and this is something I am deeply passionate about for the overall future of the sport. Gymnastics is brilliant but it can be a nightmare to watch regularly if you don't really know what's going on. The intricacies of the skills and the scoring is virtually impossible for someone to understand if they don't have an above average knowledge of the sport. Compare that with football, which the casual observer will easily see that it is about getting the ball in the other team's goal and the team that does that the most wins – simple. Yet with gymnastics, the judging is constantly changing and for someone to understand why someone has scored 15.60 and another person 14.80 would take hours of breaking down complicated rules for them. If our sport is to become something bigger than just something people are fascinated by at an Olympic Games, then we have to change the sport. Gymnastics has to find a way to capture a more mainstream audience.

There are so many comparisons that I can use to make this point. Take cricket, which is another sport I love and was really good at as a kid. I love Test Cricket – it is so multi-layered that you can be fascinated by it for five days at a time, but that is because I grew up with the sport. A casual observer can find it too complicated and slow. So, guess what? Cricket developed Twenty20 Cricket which has now revolutionised the sport. It is shorter, simpler and with more eye-catching action that anyone can admire. It has hit a bigger mainstream audience with this format and the top players are earnings huge sums of money.

Darts is another example. Before Barry Hearn took on darts it was a relatively niche sport, but Barry brought a format of it to a much bigger audience. The Premier League of Darts or the World Championships at Alexandra Palace are more than just about the darts now, they are an entertainment show! People, who thirty years ago would never have even dreamt of it, have started going to the darts. As a result, the sport has been transformed into a commercial machine with players earnings good sums of money and broadcasters giving it the attention it deserves.

This is what gymnastics needs to do, and now!

There is always resistance to change, especially from people trying to retain power, and I believe that has existed within British Gymnastics in recent years. However, gymnastics can go through a similar change to cricket. Test Cricket wasn't abandoned when Twenty20 Cricket arrived, they co-exist. The traditional scoring and competitions for gymnastics can definitely still stay but there needs to be a newer version created that captures people's imaginations. And take into account how much gymnastics has got going for it as a sport compared to others – firstly, gymnasts look physically incredible! The skills we perform are breathtaking and there is danger everywhere when we do what we do. Like I said earlier, it is like superhumans showing off! A gymnastics audience has so much to enjoy in the sport, we just have to make it simpler to understand and in a format that generates fast excitement for a live and TV audience. How slow a current gymnastics event is actually a big surprise to anyone new to the sport.

What I have accomplished with my content can be done on a broader level with gymnastics. Let's allow the sport to bloom and take it to the next level. It is going to need people making decisions who are brave and broad thinking, but it is all possible. We need to truly entertain people in a way that fits somewhere between where we are now and TV shows like Gladiators and Ninja Warrior. Of course, as part of this, I would love to see elite gymnasts earn the money that I believe their skills truly deserve. The harsh reality is that even with all the recent success in British gymnastics, few gymnasts have made significant commercial gains off the back of it – me, Louis Smith, Max Whitlock and Beth Tweddle. That is really not a lot in comparison to the medals won in recent years. I feel the sport needs to do better for its best gymnasts. But then look at British Gymnastics itself and the number of sponsors it has attracted over the years – nowhere near enough. Once upon a time, Jane Allen lazily offered me £200 to come into a meeting with Gymshark to try and convince them to become a British Gymnastics sponsor, which pretty much summed up the level of professionalism shown by her on a commercial level. Given the intensity that medals are chased to earn UK Sport funding, there have been so many commercial opportunities missed. There was too much protection placed on retaining power and credibility for successes at major events to seriously consider what was best for the future of the sport and those that dedicate their lives to it. Jane always came up with a list of reasons why the sport couldn't make a change but, in my opinion, they were just glorified excuses for her to use in order to maintain her power on the sport.

I appreciate Barry Hearn's company, Matchroom, has made an attempt at these sorts of ideas with the World Cup of Gymnastics, but I believe so much more can be done. As you can probably tell by now, I am deeply passionate about all of this and have some strong ideas on it. I would love to tell you all my ideas in this book, but I am going to keep them secret until I can be a big part of the reason that they become reality!

Gymnastics is already brilliant, but it has so much untapped potential at the moment. Once that potential is fully realised, the landscape for the sport will be changed forever and everyone from gymnasts, coaches and administrators will benefit from it.

It is going to take brave people to drive this forward and I am going to be one of them!

Chapter 17

Now

Sometimes it feels as if a lot has happened to me during my twenty-five years on this earth!

This book has allowed me to reflect on all of it. Within a five-year period, I have had some enormous highs matched by some desperate lows, both in and out of the gym. I have pushed the boundaries of what people believed is possible and now I sit outside the elite programme of gymnastics in this country. Regardless of all of this, I genuinely feel I have only just got started in what I want to achieve.

In my world and the people that I surround myself with, anything is possible. If I make the progress that I have made in the last five years at the same pace for the next five to ten years, then hold tight folks, there is a lot more to come!

These are my goals:

- Nile Wilson Gymnastics will have an unrivalled gymnastics presence in the United Kingdom; one that matches anything achieved in the fitness industry.
- I will be one of the most successful content creators in this country.
- I will create a mind-blowing live experience for people to watch gymnastics.
- I will continue to be a spokesman for our incredible sport of gymnastics and how gymnasts are treated.
- I will continually attract new audiences to gymnastics.

- Maybe even more importantly, I will continue to work on myself to overcome the mental health challenges I have and be the best possible version of myself that I can be.
- I will always strive to inspire.

Just remember, anything is possible guys!

Thank you for continuing to be part of my journey.

Acknowledgements

Mum and Dad - Thank you for being my Mum and Dad, always. Life has thrown some weird and wonderful things at me and you have always been there to hold my hand and give me every ounce or your unconditional love. I'm sorry for being the nightmare child!

Luke Sutton – Thank you for inspiring me to become a better human being every single day! You always have been, and always will be, way more than my 'manager' and I hope one day to be even half the man you are. I'm excited to see what we can achieve in this life, in and out of business.

Joanna – Thank you for being my number one fan and the 'bestest sister in the whole wide world'. You always say 'I just want to be like my big brother Nile', but the truth is I've always wanted to be just like my baby sister Joanna. Here's to Oblivion in everything we do.

Barry Collie, Dave Murray and Moussa Hamani – Thank you for believing in me even when I didn't believe in myself. Our time in the gym trying to master all those gymnastics tricks was always my happiest place! I hope you cherish those special moments we had on the competition floor! I know I do.

Gill Davy – Thank you for fixing me and unfortunately having to do it too much, ha ha. Regardless of every niggle, minor and major injury, my Monday morning physio sessions were some of the most important moments of my life! You helped me more than you know, in and out of sport.

Medical team – Every doctor, physiotherapist, psychologist and nutritionist that I've have crossed paths with (you know who you are), it's been an absolute pleasure and thank you for your unwavering support! I was the crazy one, and out of all the gymnasts I was definitely the one who saw you guys the most! But without you, I wouldn't be where I am today.

Michael Finnigan – Thank you for seeing something in that 18-year-old lad. Honestly, to have you as a mentor completely changed my life and I'm so proud to be working with you! Let's keep dreaming.

Luke Stoney and Ashley Watson – Thank you for being my best friends. When I need £1 and you've only got 50p, you borrow 50p to give me £1. That's the way it's always been and the way it always will be. Through thick and thin we are the three musketeers.

Men's Olympic Top Squad – You know who every single one of you are, thank you for being my biggest inspirations. We've shared memories together that less that 0.000001 per cent of this planet ever get to experience. The flips in the gym were fun, competing on the battlefield was even more fun, but it's the brotherhood we share that I will cherish forever.